Lessons from Afghanistan

by David Fleishhacker

DF publications

© 2001 by David Fleishhacker.

Published by DF Publications, DfLessons@aol.com.

Cover: the great ancient arch at Qaleh Bist, near Lashkar Gah (photograph by the author).

ISBN 0-9717176-0-5

Contents

Introduction: Why This Book Came To Be   1

A Preface: Where Is Everybody?   7

Part I: Nine Americans in Kabul

Why We Went 13

Kabul, 1962 17

How We Lived 22

The Land of Nothing 27

Food 32

Entertainment 39

Enshalla 46

Pay No Attention 50

Is This a Teacher? 54

Yes It Is, No It Isn't 59

Zenda-ba-Non 65

Masdurat 71

Travel at the Speed of a Camel 77

Mazar-i-Sharif 83

On the Road Again 92

Part II: What We Need to Learn

Politics as Unusual 99

Working with Washington 107

Dope 114

Time 119

Hats 126

Standing in Line 130
The Gods Must Be Crazy 136
Terrorism Began With Statues 144
Lessons 149

Acknowledgments

The friendships and support, many years ago, of our Peace Corps Director in Kabul, Bob Steiner, and his entire family

The other eight volunteers of Afghan I: Frank, Bob, Rosalind, Jan, Jill, Dolores, and the two Dorothys,

The training and friendship Afghan I experienced years ago from Jim Pence, Dr. Clarence Linton Dr. Harold Amoss, and that great expert on Afghanistan, the late Dr. Louis Dupree,

Recent information and insights from Jason Elliot's A Distant Light and Larry P. Goodson's Afghanistan's Endless War,

Useful information and suggestions I received from various people while I was writing and hoping to publish this, especially from Elaine Petrocelli of Book Passage,

My family's allowing me to indulge in an expenditure of time and money to satisfy my own ego,

My wife, who demonstrates strength and courage, as well patience with all my behaviors, some of which she tolerates and others which she has forgiven,

My cousin Gail, who read the book, liked it, and told me so,

The people of Afghanistan, who endure.

Why This Book Came To Be

THE WORLD HAS CHANGED, BUT LOOKING FORWARD demands looking backward. One does not step into traffic without glancing in both directions, yet Americans, as this book will demonstrate, often act as if they could shape their futures without considering their past. This book is a memoir, and much of it may entertain the reader, but it also records lessons from the past which are needed now more than ever.

September 11, 2001, will be a milestone in American history. It marks the date when a national desire to retreat into isolationism, brought on by self-doubt and disillusion following the folly of Vietnam, suddenly ended. As on December 7, 1941, Americans awoke to the realization that however much they desired to pursue peace and prosperity behind their borders, their safety and security would demand direct involvement with distant lands and issues of international concern.

My experience in Afghanistan predated Vietnam; it occurred during the Cold War, a time when thinking Americans assumed that we were engaged in and needed to be informed about every corner of the globe. The Peace Corps, in 1962, was one small part of that engagement, and some of us decided to enlighten ourselves by service in that new effort.

When I returned from duty in 1964, there was a certain degree of interest in the Peace Corps, and I was invited to speak and show slides on several occasions. I enjoyed doing that. Much of this book might have been written thirty-five years ago, had I then the inclination to write and the time away from work to do so. But it would have been a very different book.

In any event, I got married and resumed my teaching career; and then the Vietnam War broke out, and Americans had little interest in the Peace Corps or a central Asian country called Afghanistan which seemed far from American concerns.

So I put away my notes, slides, and souvenirs, and eventually became head of an independent school, and a father, and twenty-five years later I retired, then went back to work again and retired again, and found I had leisure time. And by then I had begun writing funny little verses and Christmas letters and lots of other stuff, using a computer.

Before the computer age, I had never enjoyed writing, since my eye-hand coordination is so poor that writing manually is slow, with results painful to decipher. Typing was not much easier. It was only when my wife bought me my first little white Apple IIc that I discovered how easy it is to write when typing errors can easily be corrected and ideas smoothly moved around. For the first time I discovered that I enjoyed writing, plunging in and letting ideas flow and later putting everything in order, adding and subtracting sections as necessary. I started writing as part of my daily job as a school head and found that others enjoyed reading what I wrote.

Still, this book would never have been written had it not been for the attack of September 11 that suddenly brought Afghanistan into American consciousness. Coincidentally, just a few weeks earlier I happened to read the only recent one, A Distant Light by Jason Elliot, and so as the names "Taliban" and "Kabul" and "Mazar-I-Sharif" suddenly appeared in my morning paper every day, I was already primed to revisit a nearly forgotten part of my life. I found that bookstores quickly sold out of anything about Islam. They did not sell out of books on Afghanistan, since there had never been any to buy. I was intrigued to discover that nothing was available for the average reader about that country, nor was it possible to find material which might help Americans understand the fundamental differences in the cultures of lands like Afghanistan and our own, so that the daily events recorded in the newspaper could be read with any real understanding of what was going on.

I was asked by a local women's club to speak at a luncheon about Afghanistan, and I dragged out my old slides and my old diary and discovered a dusty cardboard box where I had, thirty years before, put away all my teaching materials, newspaper clippings, and other records of my stay in that far land. Then I found a cache of letters.

My mother was a collector. She kept every letter her father had sent her when she was a young girl in school in Paris. She kept every letter her children wrote to her. At her death I had reclaimed a box of such letters and put it away in my basement. And there they were, when I went to look for the other materials: forty-six letters I wrote over two years, recounting details I had long forgotten of an adventure that shaped my life in a land which now was suddenly a new enigma for a new generation of Americans.

I had an agent for another book, and I asked her if she thought it might be worthwhile for me to try to produce a "quickie" book on Afghanistan, given the absence of anything much on the market outside of old, serious, scholarly material. She told me to forget it. Publishing houses had staff to produce quickie books. Reminiscences would have little if any appeal to the general public.

I took her advice to heart, for about a day. Then I decided to write this book anyway, for my children if for no one else.

And for myself. I had never set down my thoughts about that amazing time in that unique country since those letters and that diary. Yet except for boarding school and college, I had never lived as long as two years anywhere but in San Francisco, where I was born and raised (as were my parents and grandparents, and where my children and grandchildren live today). Afghanistan was the closest thing to a second home I would ever know. The people there were universally kind to me, and my stay there was a special interlude that changed the rest of my life in important ways. I owed it to myself, and to the people of Afghanistan, those whom I knew (most of whom must be dead) and those I never knew, to express what I have not seen expressed by others.

Soon after September 11, I heard calls for our troops to bomb Afghanistan back into the Stone Age. I heard others claim that Afghanistan was already back in the Stone Age. I read all the articles I could find about the events there and was struck by the lack of deep understanding of Afghan geography, history and culture which reflected how great the distance had grown between our people, even our most educated citizens, and the realities of life in other parts of the world.

I felt a need to explain Afghanistan to Americans and, as I sat down and started to do that, I found myself explaining America to myself.

Afghanistan is not in the Stone Age. It once contained centers of enlightened culture at a time when North America had not emerged from the Stone Age and Europe had descended into a period of darkness similar to that which has fallen upon Afghanistan today. Even a generation ago, Afghanistan had a more enlightened government and was less convulsed by hatred than many of its supposedly civilized neighbors. It was never a technologically sophisticated land, but its people were better fed, less brutalized, and generally happier than many who, at that time, suffered under the oppressions of totalitarian regimes to their north and east.

Afghanistan has nothing, really, to do with Bin Laden, or other terrorists groups that make up the foreign elements hiding out in its mountains. It does have fundamentalist religious madmen, as does our own nation. The small gangs of bandits known as the Taliban, who controlled much of the country for half a decade, were influenced by a perverted distortion of Islam. But the Taliban was not Afghanistan, any more than the KKK or the Aryan Brotherhood are America. If Afghanistan had roads and communication and an economy like ours, the Taliban would never have been able to gain control. If a devastating war had not put the weapons of modern war into their hands, they could not have maintained control for a few years.

"They cannot maintain it much longer," I wrote, in September 2001, a prediction that came true faster than I could have guessed. By the time I began to edit this book, Kabul had fallen. Soon a new regime would be in titular control of the country, but the nature of that regime and whether it, in turn, will survive long, remains unpredictable. Afghanistan has been conquered many times, but it has never been effectively governed.

In any case, change in governance of Afghanistan will not stop terrorism, which will move to other lands. In order eventually to end terrorism, more needs to be done than to eliminate terrorists in one country. That is the subject of some other book. Yet unless can we can gain greater knowledge of the day-to-day lives of peoples like those who live in Afghanistan, we will have no possibility of responding intelligently to what has become an immediate and fundamental threat to civilization.

This book is about a country I love, what it once was like, and what we need to understand in order to help it revive. Afghanistan has just undergone one more convulsion of revolution and war, and the U.S. can become its destroyer or its savior. In order to breathe life into that wounded land, many nations will have to combine efforts and abandon rivalries. The wisdom with which we deal with the people of Afghanistan and other countries will, to a great extent, determine the way America is perceived and, more important, be a measure of our right to continue to influence the future.

Terrorists who would destroy America have no justification for their abominable acts, which stem from ignorance and prejudice. Americans, in response, need to act from understanding and tolerance. This book is one small attempt on the part of one American to broaden that understanding and tolerance in the interest of greater enlightenment, not for Afghans, but for Americans, whose power in the world, without greater enlightenment, cannot be used as it must be: to maintain our own freedom and security and that of our children by seeking to further human progress everywhere.

6

Where Is Everybody?

I T HAD BEEN NEARLY FORTY YEARS SINCE I LIVED IN Afghanistan,more than half a lifetime ago. For two months in the fall of 2001, I awoke every day and read about bombs and troops and starving people there, and I could not help but be aroused by anger and pity. Then I read comments by journalists and letters to the editor, mostly by well-meaning people, and I was aroused by recognizing how uninformed and narrow their viewpoints were and how unprepared we all are, as a nation, to confront and understand that part of the world.

What could I have learned so long ago which might be relevant in the circumstances we face today?

Well, let's start with the simple question: How many people live in Afghanistan?

Every news report I heard or read spoke of the drought and the possible military assault faced by 25 million people in that country (or 21 million, or even 27 million). It is a country a bit smaller than Texas, with a landscape that resembles Nevada. Do 25 million people live there, and why do we think so?

When I was training for the Peace Corps, one of the first "facts" we were given was that the population was about 12 million people. The second fact presented to us was that the figure was a rough estimate that nobody who had lived in the country for very long thought was vaguely close to correct. There had never been a real census in Afghanistan, nor has there been one since. The borders have always been porous. The figure of 12 million, as far as anyone could tell, was an estimate based on the fact that someone had estimated a figure of 6 million, or 8 million, of some other million people at some time in the past, and that someone else had projected a population growth similar to what occurs in other countries.

During the time I lived in Afghanistan, the question kept coming up. I even discussed it with Afghan friends, none of whom had any strong opinion about what the population of their country might be and none of whom thought that the figure of 12 million was accurate.

I lived in the capital, Kabul, where the population was estimated to be about 300,000. From my experience living there, that number seemed to be about as right as any. The second largest city in the country was Kandahar, estimated population 75,000. I spent several months in another large city, Mazar-i-Sharif, where the population might have been 30,000. There were four or five other cities in the country. So if one added up the population of all the cities and towns in Afghanistan, one might find one million people. Maybe.

Where were the other 11 million people?

I traveled in Afghanistan on several occasions. I saw some fertile valleys with small farms. I saw treeless mountains, and barren, deserted plains. I saw true deserts; one large section of the country is called the Dasht-i-Margo, or Desert of Death, and it is well named. As I said, the country looks like Nevada. Not many people can scratch out a living in most of Nevada, and not many people could do any better in most of Afghanistan.

So maybe there were 12 million people there, somewhere, about 11 million of them unnoticed. Or maybe the number was just made up and unchallenged because to get an accurate count someone would have to spend a great deal of time and money traveling around a country with no good roads, employing people trained to do such surveys where no such people exist, and identifying people who do often do not have a fixed residence, do not generally use last names, do not have any understanding of or interest in statistics, and would regard the question as hopelessly silly and unanswerable.

Nevada has a population of just over 2 million, but most of that is in Las Vegas and Reno. There is no city anything like Las Vegas in Afghanistan. Take the current figure of 2 million population for Kabul, which you will find if you seek this information on-line. Find a picture, anywhere, of Kabul. Two million people there?

The same can be said for all the population figures one will find for Afghan cities: they seem to be projections based on taking highly questionable estimates made in 1979 and projecting assumed increases, in spite of two decades of war, a terrible rate of infant mortality, and massive migrations. Some of these projections show increases of 500%. Where in the world would all these people have come from? What supports them? More important, where would the capital to build these cities come from? American suburbs have sprung up in recent decades around malls and shopping centers, their development fueled by a thriving consumerist economy. There are no malls in Afghanistan, and there is no capital to create them or to build new housing.

Texas, with an area comparable to that of Afghanistan, has a population of 21 million. Texas has cities like Dallas, Fort Worth, Houston, and El Paso. Texas has dozens of smaller cities and large towns. Afghanistan has neither huge cities nor many small towns.

Even assuming that the highly doubtful figures one can find listed for the population of Afghan cities are more than rough guesses, the total population of the 20 largest cities would be under 5 million. That would mean that 15 to 20 million people are living out in the "countryside" on land which is estimated to be only one to five percent arable. What are those people doing to stay alive?

For all these reason, the assumption that Afghanistan has a population larger than that of Texas is untenable. Yet our government acts on that assumption. Aid is based on that assumption. It is likely that the inflated figures have origins in the need for aid, so that it may turn out to be a blessing that we attempt to supply food for millions of people who may not live there. Those who do live there need all we can spare. But any military plans or humanitarian efforts based on the population figures generally cited are almost certainly built on false assumptions.

For Americans, who live in a country that could not exist without technology, the question of how many people live somewhere seems not only an essential piece of information but one that is easily ascertainable. Our Constitution requires that we count our people every decade, and we have done that for over two centuries. Our census may have some major inaccuracies, but it does have a sound basis.

Afghanistan does not have a constitution. It has never, really, had a stable government, or a census, or a functioning transportation system, or a common language. It is in many ways an artificial country, created by other powers for reasons of their own. Most people there do not think about the world the way we think about it because it is not the same world.

That is the real point of confronting such a basic concept as a country's population. It seems to Americans as if we should know what it is. But we do not. We are in the dark about this and much, much more.

One has to live in such a country for a while to understand the profound differences not only in day-to-day life but in perception of what life is. I lived there for two years. When I hear people speak about it, even highly educated people, I wonder if they have any understanding about how unprepared they are to form opinions about what is so remote from their experience and sensibilities.

This book may be nearly forty years late, but I haven't found anything in bookstores that confronts our overwhelming ignorance of the profound differences between our land and others. We assume we know much about the world. Our assumptions seem reasonable, to us. But our way of looking at the world is based on our own experience, and our experience of something as simple as counting population fails us when we apply it here.

We also have faith in statistics and facts, orderly records to assist us in planning for the future. Our facts are often simply wrong, and our faith in our ability to plan the future is, we sometimes discover, no more than faith. We need to step back and examine some of our most fundamental assumptions of our power to shape the world, assumptions that are at least questionable and, in the eyes of many other nations, arrogant. Our pride and certainty has already alienated us from much of the world. The lessons one learns from living in another culture cannot be learned simply by reading about them or by visiting for a few days or weeks. Even a trained reporter has not ordinarily been taught to understand the culture being reported. No matter how long one visits another country, a visitor has a limited perspective. Living and working in an unfamiliar culture for a year or two provides a different level of understanding and appreciation of critical cultural.

So perhaps this book can recall how a few Americans once had experiences very different from what is familiar to most of us and thereby suggest some starting points for considering how to proceed in Afghanistan and elsewhere, in order to save us all from the potentially horrifying results of the folly which can result from decades of isolation from the world beyond our borders.

12

Why We Went

WE WEREN'T ALL DO-GOODER IDEALISTS THOSE first years of the Peace Corps. This was pre-Vietnam; there hadn't been any wars to protest against, nor did anyone other than hard-core communists, pacifists, or one world idealists strongly object to American actions in the Cold War. We enlisted in the Peace Corps in those first years because of the charisma of John F. Kennedy, whose brainchild it was, because of our desire to find something challenging to do before starting a career, or because of simple, personal, selfish reasons. In my case, it was mostly the last of those.

I had been deferred from the draft because of a hyperactive thyroid, but now that my thyroid had been calmed (actually, 95% removed), my draft board had made it clear that I would not be deferred again. Hence, I could not continue as a teacher at the school where I had been employed for two years; my inevitable departure in the middle of the second semester would have been too disruptive. I had decided to return to graduate school. I was certain I could be deferred for at least the few months needed to finish one year's study.

It was on the Berkeley campus that I heard a touring Sargent Shriver speak about the Peace Corps. It sounded like a better way to spend my time than continuing my graduate studies, which I found of little interest, or ending up as a clerk-typist somewhere on an Army base, which is what people with my educational background generally became after being drafted. There was no assurance that I would be permanently exempt from the draft, but it seemed likely that I would be too old for the draft once I had completed Peace Corps service. Meanwhile, deferment was not promised but seemed likely. I sent in my name.

By the time a response came in the mail, I was already well into the semester's work, so when I was offered a chance to serve in Thailand, although that sounded fascinating, I asked to be deferred from Peace Corps service until June. And that's how I ended up in June of 1962, training at Georgetown University as part of the first Peace Corps group to serve in Afghanistan.

We were the smallest group in Peace Corps history. Afghanistan was the only truly neutral country on the Soviet border, and the government there was walking a tightrope between the East and the West, carefully balancing aid from both camps. Russians were building roads and laying lines for natural gas in the north; the U.S. was building roads and assisting farming in the south. The Russians were providing military expertise; the Americans were helping the Ministries of Economics and Education. Hence, the Afghans feared that anticipating fifty to one hundred Peace Corps volunteers about to descend on their country, as was occurring in other countries, would upset their northern neighbors. They asked for six teachers, four nurses, and two mechanics, and the Peace Corps, simply wanting to get a foot in the door, set out to identify fifteen candidates for those twelve positions. They found fourteen. Nine of us eventually got to Afghanistan.

It was during our two-month training period that I began to realize that my motives for joining the Peace Corps were no more or less noble than those of the other volunteers.

Most of us were in our early twenties. There was also one retired couple, a very sweet pair of elderly teachers whom the rest of us worried about. We thought the assignment would be rigorous, and we doubted the ability of people older than ourselves to handle it (now that I am over sixty, I see things somewhat differently). In any event, two weeks after we started training, they were offered regular jobs on Guam and left to take those jobs.

Another volunteer was dropped at the end of training. The rumor we heard was that he had signed up to avoid the complications of his girlfriend's pregnancy. We never learned if this were true or not. We did learn that, during training, background checks took place. Some of our neighbors and friends later told us they had been questioned by government agents; this made us feel very James Bondish. We did not need to assume that our departed fellow trainee had a dark secret; several of us had looked on with trepidation one day when, leaving a classroom, a thick trail of ants crossed our path and this particular volunteer suddenly stamped on, or rather danced on, the trail, for over a minute, squashing ants into the concrete pathway. It was one of those moments when people look at one other silently, wondering what kind of strange emotion is working itself out in a stranger's brain.

Another volunteer, a nurse, completed training but during our leave period (between the time we finished training and were to depart for Asia) she became engaged; we never saw her again. We speculated on whether she had volunteered in order to jolt her boyfriend into a decision. Out of thirteen who began training, four had already departed, and we hadn't even left Washington yet.

That's why there were only nine of us on a plane to Kabul, via Rome and Teheran, in September of 1962. I still felt a bit guilty about my own motives for becoming a volunteer. There were only three men in the group, one of whom was married (and therefore deferred from the draft) and the other of whom had already served in the army. Draft dodging, even of the sort I was engaging in, was not considered acceptable except for college students and married men at that time.

Then, not long after we had arrived in Kabul and met our on-site director, Bob Steiner, I heard him tell us all that we were there for the best possible of reasons: what he called "enlightened self-interest." All of us felt we would benefit in various ways from the experience, and that was much better than if we were a bunch of starry-eyed idealists who thought we were sacrificing ourselves. He was right, of course; people who are working in their own self-interest are less likely to abandon that work when the going gets rough.

And, on a much deeper level, we had already been made to understand during training that the Peace Corps itself was an example of enlightened self-interest on the part of our country. Whether or not we could accomplish something of value for the countries we served was problematic at best. But there was a less-advertised purpose behind the creation of the Peace Corps. Ten years later, twenty years later, and even later still, there would be thousands and thousands of Americans of all ages who had lived and worked in far distant countries with far different cultures and whose perception of the world would be altered by that experience. That core of Americans, educated by an experience like no other, would change how America viewed the world. It was a huge experiment in national adult education, and to a large extent it has worked. I have met many former Peace Corps volunteers, but I have met none who were not profoundly changed by their two years of life in a developing country. Nor have I met any who did not have an under-standing of the world outside the United States more informed than that of most of the legislators and officials in our government.

At times like the present, people who have spent their lives in our country, often only in Washington, suddenly are empowered to create policy directing our nation's interaction with the rest of the world, of which they know so little. The leaders of other enlightened nations have far broader experience than ours with cultures outside their borders.

Americans do travel more than citizens of less affluent countries, but few actually live abroad for long. Even fewer stay any longer than they have to in lands where the standard of living is much below our own, which is to say, most countries outside Europe and Japan. When they do, they often bring their living standards with them, isolating themselves from the real lives of the people they need to know. As we enter a new era of confronting terrorism and of understanding other cultures in order to safeguard our own, I wish there were more ex-Peace Corps volunteers in our country. We do see things differently, and we see them with a vision that has been expanded exponentially by our exposure to what most Americans can only imagine, and imagine poorly.

Kabul, 1962

KABUL, IN SEPTEMBER OF 1962, WAS A CITY UNLIKE ANY I had ever seen or have seen since. A few square blocks reflected the 20th century, but most seemed to belong to the world of one hundred years earlier, and large sections would not have been out of place in the Middle Ages.

Not that anything resembled what one would then find in an American city, or any of the major cities of Europe, Africa, or Asia. The widest streets had been paved, but only recently. Behind the main streets there were narrow unpaved alleys. Along the main streets there were sidewalks, some of them paved, many not. Usually there were deep ditches on both sides of these streets, serving as gutters and to some extent as open sewers. When walking around the city, one could not help notice in vacant lots and sometimes even on dirt sidewalks what at first appeared to be dog droppings in profusion. There were very few dogs around, however. These were human.

The only paved road in the country led from a few miles north of Kabul, through the city, and then east to the Pakistan border. There were no trains in Afghanistan; there never have been any and there are none today, except for a small spur near the northern border, built by the Russians during their occupation. There was once, briefly, a streetcar in

Kabul, back in the 1920s; in 1962 it was on display near the Kabul museum.

There was one stoplight in the city, near the Kabul Hotel. There were streetlights in some areas. Traffic consisted of bicycles, donkeys or donkey carts, camels, sheep, and pedestrians, all mixed together, and a few cars, mostly Russian ones.

There was one modern hotel. There was one modern restaurant. There were perhaps a dozen or so buildings of more than two stories. There were, of course, no department stores; there were really no stores at all that would resemble what one would expect to find in a major city. There were shops of varying types, but these were always one-room affairs. One could find, for example, a shop near the Kabul hotel which had a dozen or so appliances on display, small refrigerators and radios, mostly German. One could find many shops with native Afghan clothing, intended for the few tourists who drifted through. There was one airline office, for Ariana Afghan airlines, a dusty room with a desk and a few chairs. There were some moderately imposing government buildings, built in a nineteenth-century style resembling offices in provincial Russia.

The Kabul Hotel was hardly luxurious but it was clean and comfortable, comparable to a first-class hotel (as contrasted with a luxury hotel) in Europe. Because of normal government red tape and delays, no housing had been found for us when we arrived in mid-September, so of necessity we were housed in the hotel. After having been assured that we would be living much as the native population lived, this was disconcerting for us; the Kabul Hotel was not grand by western standards, but it was the grandest hotel within hundreds of miles. It had marble floors and walls. The furniture was stolid and ugly, but comfortable. The rooms had excellent bath facilities. Breakfast was served daily in a pleasant dining room, with ample coffee, tea, cereals, toast, and eggs, served by waiters eager to learn and eager to please. We were comfortable, but we felt like tourists, and that was the last thing we wanted.

Lacking kitchens of our own, we had to eat out (except when invited to American or Afghan homes, as we often were), and that meant eating at the Khyber restaurant one block away. The Khyber was a sort of cafeteria, with a choice of stews, potatoes, and vegetables created for Western tastes, and its offerings, if essentially unchanging, were hearty and palatable. On certain occasions they offered something resembling a steak, probably the filet, which had been thoroughly pounded in order to tenderize it, and then broiled. It wasn't at all bad.

The chefs at the Khyber did a decent job of approximating Western dishes. It was not haute cuisine, but it was solid fare, and we continued to eat there on occasion even when we were established in our own homes. Besides lamb dishes, sometimes one could have Cram Steak or Chicken Fagazy, and at other times the menu featured Meat Luves, Bouling Beef, or Beef Lives. These were, of course, crumb steak (the pounded meat mentioned above, in a crumb batter), chicken fricassee, meat loaf, boiled beef, and beef liver.

The hotel and restaurant, along with several government buildings, were near Pushtunistan Square, one center of the modern city. The city, like the country of which it is the capital, did not really have a center. The Kabul River divides the north of the city from the south. Even more is it divided, east from west, by high mountains, with old walls dating from the times of Buddhist resistance to Islamic invaders. Thus, the city has a dumbbell shape, with a narrow waist where the river cuts through a gorge in those mountains. Much of the modern city spreads out in a fan to the east of that constriction. There, to the south of Pushtunistan Square, there was a broad, east-west street, the Jade Maiwand, marking the site of the old bazaar burned by the British a century before. From Pushtunistan Square north led the road to the airport and several foreign embassies. The new American embassy, abandoned when the Russians invaded, and burned in September of 2001, would later be built on that road, but in 1962 it was in Share Nau, or the "New City" to the northeast, as was the city's Park, the Park Theater, a new mosque, and many new homes.

The western parts of Kabul, on the other side of the gorge, were known as Karte Char and Karte Se, or the "Fourth district" and "Third district." These were mostly older mud-brick residential areas, except for Kabul University, which lay in the shadow of the mountains to its north. Rising up the mountain slopes were tiers of houses, accessible only by narrow, steep alleys and pathways.

Deeper into the city, in level areas, there were many shops, nearly identical ones displaying mountains of fruits and vegetables, neatly piled up every morning and put away every evening. There were butcher shops with meat hanging from hooks on display. There were shops with dried fruits, nuts, and spices. There were several shops with canned goods imported from Europe, brought in by truck from Iran or smuggled up from Pakistan. There were metalwork shops and carpenter shops and every other kind of shop where human labor could be turned into relatively crude household goods. There were shops with cheap imported goods from China and Japan. There was virtually nothing for sale manufactured in Afghanistan because there were essentially no factories. We were given a tour of a new textile factory north of the city, and I later learned of other textile factories in the northern city of Kunduz, but other than that there was no sign of heavy industry, and light industry meant hand-manufactured goods exclusively.

Unlike other cities in Afghanistan, most of the houses had electricity, and many of the streets were lit, and so at night it was safe and easy to walk, as people do in other large cities today. The freedom to spend time out of doors at night is a very modern freedom, one which is less common than we, who live in cities of the West, may recognize. Without exterior lighting, people must stay in their homes for most of their lives after the sun sets. That was still the case in most of Afghanistan, even in other cities, where lighting was limited to relatively few streets. Kabul was therefore years ahead of other parts of the country, if not in buildings and amenities, at least in some freedoms people there could enjoy.

That was Kabul in 1962. During the next two years, we saw surprising changes, albeit on a modest scale. A new hotel, the Spinzar, was under construction; progress, by Western standards, came slowly in Kabul, but the hotel was almost complete when I left in 1964, and there were rumors of the new Intercontinental Hotel, later to be the only hotel for foreign visitors. A new Western-style restaurant also opened, but I only went there once, at invitation, because Peace Corps volunteers were supposed to avoid living a Western life style as much as possible. A number of new buildings went up near Pushtunistan Square and on the road to the airport. Some bridges across the Kabul River were widened. Things were moving along, and the city was definitely cleaner and newer than it had been two years before. Still, when I arrived in Teheran on my way home, I experienced my first instance of culture shock. I went into an airline office to confirm a ticket and, finding it carpeted, with modern lighting and furniture (resembling no office I had seen for two years), I assumed I was in the wrong place. There was no office of any kind I had seen in Afghanistan as nicely, cleanly, and comfortably furnished as that simple Teheran airline office.

Since then, I have not been back, so I do not really know exactly how Kabul has changed. But I have seen films and photos. All of them suggest that the wars of the last decades have reduced Kabul to desperate conditions. Most houses in Kabul were of mud-brick construction; modern weaponry has transformed many of these to powder. Government buildings were mostly concrete, but those buildings have been targets of assault by one regime after another. I have glimpsed a few images of the city today. Those pictures show little but rubble and concrete shells, although there must be areas where less destruction has occurred, or the city would be empty.

For those who can only imagine what it must be like today, I suggest that you do not imagine London after the blitz, or the cities of Germany after World War II, for Kabul had never resembled those cities before their destruction. At its peak, it may have approached what London or Paris looked like in 1500. Imagine those cities, at that time, and then imagine the effects on them of modern land-based warfare and bombing raids. That must be Kabul today.

Kabul, from all reports, is still the only large city in Afghanistan. It was the devastating street fighting between neighborhood warlords that took place after the Russians left, not the American bombing campaign, which destroyed so much of the city. In spite of propaganda to the contrary, the recent American bombing and subsequent occupation of the city by the Northern Alliance does not seem to have caused much destruction, and the loss of life reported was far less than that caused by some of the brutal massacres under the Taliban. But it is, and will be for many years, a fundamentally wounded city, with mostly broken buildings and broken lives.

How We Lived

▼▼▼▼▼▼

WE GOT TO KNOW OTHER PARTS OF THE CITY, WHERE we lived and worked, during the next year, but for our first weeks in Kabul we had not yet received work assignments and spent most of our time still training. In fact, some of us would have been training for weeks, under a group from Columbia Teachers' College already working at Afghan schools as part of a government AID program, had we not rebelled.

Our rebellion stemmed from the first day when we were handed a syllabus of what was planned for our instruction by someone who then read the syllabus to us. We had been training for months in how to teach English as a foreign language, and we had no patience with anyone beginning the process all over again in typical education-school fashion, taking an hour to read an outline of a plan to us instead of just getting on with it. Look, we said, if you guys know something special from having worked here already, tell us what that is, and then get out of our way, because we're not going through TEFL instruction all over again. Our training was reduced to another two hours.

The Peace Corps, at this early stage of its existence, was still feeling its way, and we were part of those tentative explorations. The original mandate of the Peace Corps was that volunteers would go to foreign lands, what were then called "third world" or "underdeveloped" countries (soon to be called by the more politically correct designation of "developing" countries), live as the native population lived, be paid no more than what would support basic needs, and thus be something far different from those who worked in these lands at U.S. wages and with U.S. stipends and thus could live not only as well as they would at home but in luxury, given the huge difference in the cost of living. These were the people often called "ugly Americans" (although the book of that name actually used the name in a very different context). Then, as is still the case today, Americans felt guilty about their affluence, and about displaying it when working in countries where poverty was the norm. We were to be examples of Americans who could live in the same manner as the native population and thereby demonstrate our virtue, our compassion, and our desire to share a common destiny with all other nations. Well, with non-communist nations, anyway.

It took weeks to even begin to figure out what that really meant, and Bob Steiner, our director, spent long hours meeting with Afghan officials and speaking with bureaucrats in Washington trying to thrash out the details. For example, Washington had ideas about what kinds of housing would be appropriate, ideas that had nothing to do with actual choices available to us. Our director kept searching for housing to please Washington, and failing to find any, which was why some of were still at the Kabul hotel six weeks after we arrived.

Choosing housing turned out to be the thorniest issue. Peace Corps Washington wanted us to live in five different houses all over the city (to avoid the possibility that we would cluster together and not become involved with the native population). But houses in the capital were not designed for one or two people; Afghans do not live that way. Nor was the native population going to mingle with us, outside of work, for some time to come. Our work was mostly in one part of the city, so living far from our work would create pointless travel around a city where travel was difficult at best. We eventually divided up in three homes separated by only a few blocks, with three nurses and one female teacher in one large house, our married couple, the Pearsons, in another, and the two single males (our mechanic Frank Brechin, and me) in an apartment above some shops. So we were living like the native population. Some of them.

There was still the question as to what degree our lives should resemble that of the native population. Most Afghans suffered from chronic dysentery. If we did not take precautions, we would all get dysentery. If we did not take appropriate medicines unavailable to most Afghans, we would still get dysentery. What good would that do anyone? So of course we boiled our water and were treated with appropriate prophylactic medicine. (I was diagnosed with dysentery anyway, when I finished my service there, but fortunately it never caused me any serious problems.)

Still, most of the native population, those who had jobs like ours, lived in much poorer houses than we did. Yet they had families, and friends, and neighbors who knew them. If they got sick, there was someone to take care of them. Someone in the family cooked for them, and shopped for them, and provided companionship. We had no roots in Kabul, and at that time the unofficial government policy was that Afghans should not immediately visit us, or hang around with us, or invite us to their homes. Our houses were watched, or at least observed. This was a police state, if a fairly benign one. Afghans are a naturally hospitable and friendly people, but those who lived in Kabul knew that their actions were not entirely free, and cozying up to the latest batch of foreigners in town was not necessarily prudent. "Living like the native population" was not an option.

So the question remained as to which part of the native population our lives should parallel? Very soon it was determined that each of our households could, and should, employ a native servant. At first blush, this sounded like the opposite of everything the Peace Corps stood for. At second thought, it made complete sense. Many Afghan households, even those of modest means, had servants. Even some servants had servants. It took hours to prepare simple meals, as Frank and I learned after our first attempt to make a pot roast with a piece of local mutton. We steamed it in a pressure cooker for three hours only to discover that it was still too tough to cut with a knife. Both beef and mutton needed daylong simmering to become tender enough for human consumption. Chicken was another matter; it was generally tender enough to eat, but that was because chickens were sold live, since there was no way to preserve them, and they could not hang and cure like beef. That meant that if you wanted to eat chicken you had to buy a live one and then find a mullah to say the appropriate prayers while its neck was cut, then pluck it, clean it, and cook it. Our fellow Afghan teachers did not buy, pluck, clean, and cook their own chickens, or they would not have had time to teach. Neither would we. So a servant made absolute sense.

Moreover, had we lived without a servant, in the manner of the very poorest Afghans, our status would have been reduced to such a low level that we would have been perceived as fools or the dregs of our own society. Our ability to present ourselves as teachers would have been permanently undermined. This was not an egalitarian society, and part of our effectiveness came from our status as foreigners, demonstrating by the way we lived that education was something that could lead to upper-class comforts. We had to walk a fine line between flaunting unjustified privilege and hypocritically living as if we were impoverished natives.

As it turned out, what most distinguished us from other Americans was our transportation. For several days we used native buses to get across town from the Kabul Hotel to the offices of the Columbia Teachers' project in Karte Char. The city buses were exactly as one might imagine: packed to the limit, standing room only, slow, lurching and smelly, something any Westerner would avoid at all costs. We rode them, and people noticed. Hardly any Americans had ever entered a Kabul bus, for Americans had cars, or friends with cars, and if they didn't, there were a few taxis in town. English nationals, French nationals, and German nationals, a number of whom also lived in Kabul, also used cars (there was still one school with French as the foreign language of choice and one with German, these ties going back to the 1930s). There were many Russians in Kabul, but they lived all together in a compound on the west side of the city, and they generally were transported in large groups by buses of their own. (The Soviet Union, in 1962, did not trust its citizens living abroad to wander around by themselves.) So we heard, shortly after we arrived, that we were labeled as the Americans who rode buses. It was the first indication that there was something new in town.

Not long after we arrived, Bob Steiner decided that we really needed bicycles, since bus routes were few and generally would not take us to the schools, hospitals, and auto repair facility to which we were assigned. So we acquired good, sturdy English bicycles – mine was the only good bicycle I have ever owned, and the only one I have ever really used. I grew up in a hilly section of San Francisco where, as a child, the thought of riding a bicycle up or down my neighboring streets terrified me.

I never got very good at riding that bicycle; in fact, my riding was looked upon as something of a joke by the other volunteers. And riding through Kabul was an experience even for someone with much greater skill than I had. Many of the women still wore a *chadri* (or *"chowdri,"* or *"chadoor"*) when they went out of their homes. (*"Chadri"* was the word in general use for what American newspapers and television today refer to as a *"burkha,"* a word derived from Hindi instead of Persian.) A *chadri* renders peripheral vision impossible. Unless a woman walking along the sidewalk stops and turns her head more than ninety degrees before crossing the street, she will not see any oncoming traffic, and most women didn't do that. Donkeys also failed to observe bicycles driving by. Cars generally drove through crowds by sonar; that is, they honked horns to get everyone out of the way and plowed ahead. Bicycle riders, consequently, needed to ring their bells constantly to announce their progress down the street and hope that space might open for them.

All Americans have grown up familiar with automobiles. We develop an instinctive understanding of how fast they travel and how they behave. Afghans, especially those in or recently from the countryside, had grown up with donkeys and camels and sheep and were not skilled at judging how fast a car was approaching and how they should adopt their pace to account for that. Our first encounters with what I will mention often, cultural relativism, were with pedestrians who walked directly in front of moving cars or bicycles. On automobile trips outside of Kabul, we often observed how our drivers had to anticipate that men and women walking in the roadway might take unpredictable paths at any moment. Sometimes they seemed oblivious to swift-moving cars coming down the road. At other times, one could discern a "deer-in-the-headlights" (or possibly "donkey-in-the-headlights") expression come over the pedestrian's face when he spotted an approaching car, after which he would start in one direction, then change his mind and lurch the other way, and sometimes run right into the car. Most city dwellers had become accustomed to dealing with traffic, but that did not mean that the paths they took, which a bicyclist had to anticipate, would conform to our expectations.

On all but the a few wide streets, the distinction between sidewalk and vehicular thoroughfare was imaginary. Whether one walked or rode through Kabul, getting from one place to another was always an adventure. Traffic flowed wherever it flowed, and the only thing one could do was flow with it. It was not surprising that one did not see many bicyclists in the streets and that those one did see usually had battered old bikes their owners could barely control. So we became the Americans on bikes, just as we had been the Americans on buses, and I, given my unusual degree of ineptitude with bicycle riding, probably became the American on a bike who drove as badly as an Afghan from the countryside.

The Land of Nothing

A FGHAN RUGS ARE BEAUTIFUL, DURABLE, AND AS FINE as any made in Iran, Turkey, or any of the new central Asian nations. They are not especially varied in design; most are red, and most employ simple geometric patterns, but they are very fine rugs indeed. If you would like an Oriental rug or carpet, you could do no better than look for one in Afghanistan.

If you would like anything else in the way of art or handicrafts, you would be better off looking somewhere else.

The absence of marketable native Afghan products is only matched by the absence of natural resources and modern civilization. Afghanistan has a fascinating history as a crossroads, but for most of that history, other cultures passed through. There wasn't and isn't much reason to stay.

I never saw anything resembling a forest, although I did see some large pieces of lumber in one bazaar and I have read that some timber is exported to Pakistan, so there must be stands of trees somewhere. Yet all I ever saw were very slender, tall trees in a few river valleys, the trunks of which were used to support ceilings of Kabul homes. Wood is rare and expensive. Most trees were cut down centuries ago, and much of the landscape, except in a few river valleys, is moonlike from centuries of erosion.

Oil exploration has been carried out now and then in much of the country. There is no oil to be found.

A small amount of natural gas has been found in the northern parts of the country, but when I was there, gas from the Soviet Union supplied most of the country's needs. Most electricity depended on natural gas for generation, since the rivers are small and difficult to dam in all but a few cases, and there are no substantial coal beds.

There isn't much of anything else to mine, either. No gold or silver, certainly. No iron or other metal ores. There are beds of turquoise, exceptionally fine turquoise at that, but turquoise has a limited market, and extracting it in Afghanistan is done by primitive means in small amounts.

Afghan farmers do grow wheat, or at least they were able to before the wars of the 1990s destroyed so much of the land. They also grew the finest melons in the world, melons with crisp, white, sweet interiors. There are watermelons, too, quite good, but not as exceptional as the white melons. Grapes are harvested, but not for wine; this is a conservative Moslem land, and alcoholic beverages are not sold openly. There are nuts and chickpeas available. In the south, around Jalalabad, some oranges are grown, and rice. But many staples of the Afghan diet are imported: tea and rice are both brought up from Pakistan and India. And there is no food available for export; the basis of the Afghan diet is bread baked from local wheat and, when possible, mutton from local sheep. The local fat-tailed sheep also provides the fat used to cook rice, which is prepared in large, oily mountains, not in small bowls as in lands further to the East.

So there are essentially no Afghan woodsmen or miners, and small landowners are basically subsistence farmers. Still, every village has many shops, and perhaps there is where we might find a demonstration of special native crafts and skills. Woodworking, perhaps. Well, no, because there is so little wood, and it is of such poor quality. In India, especially in Kashmir, one once could find beautiful examples of inlaid boxes and well-crafted furniture. Nothing like this exists in Afghanistan. Similarly, one finds excellent brasswork in India and Pakistan, copper samovars, even decorated tinware. I never saw a single piece of native metalwork in Afghanistan which rose above the crudest level of design and detail.

Pottery, then. Actually, the village of Istalif is famous for its pottery, with a distinctive rich, deep turquoise glaze. Its fame is twofold: anyone who sees it wants a piece, and anyone who buys Istalif pottery soon discovers that it can only be placed, carefully, on display and never touched, for it is so fragile that a hard look seems to shatter it. That is why one has never seen Istalif ware unless one has visited Afghanistan; in all the years of craftsmen producing it, none has discovered how to make it durable enough to survive a trip out of the country.

There are, or were, textile mills in Afghanistan, and one could find some home-woven textiles, but most clothing worn by Afghans was made in other countries. There was, in one huge downtown serai, a collection of used Western clothing unlike anything I had ever seen: bales and bales of jackets and pants, piles of shoes, clusters of scarves and socks and shirts. It looked as if all the used clothing collected in the United States by second-hand clothing shops, but unsold, had been shipped to Kabul. I purchased a decent enough tweed jacket there for the equivalent of $2 when my own jacket had to be put aside for a few weeks because I had sent it to the cleaners; the cleaning method used in Kabul was to soak garments in some kind of fluid like carbon tetrachloride, and the garments continued to smell like gasoline for weeks, keeping friends at a distance and making the wearer dizzy.

One could also find wonderful embroidered goods of very colorful and tasteful design, slippers and vests, for both men or women. Most of us bought these, even though we had been advised not to. Our advisers were correct; the threads used to stitch them together were too weak, so they soon came apart. We had also been told that the leather portions were cured in camel urine; I cannot attest to the truth of this, but whatever they were cured in did not enhance their aroma. Since that time, I have on occasion seen Afghan embroidered goods in American stores, so I presume someone helped teach some tanners and tailors how to better create and preserve these wares, which are almost the only exportable hand work made in the country. India, by contrast, produces cottons, woolens, embroidered ware, linens, silks, and every imaginable kind of textiles, in addition to fine metalware, pottery, woodwork, and ceramics.

The one piece of clothing of quality which one could find was the karakul cap, which I will discuss in some detail in another chapter. Its absence today is deeply symbolic of the decline of the country.

Even when it came to art and music, Afghanistan was essentially a barren land. I saw some gorgeous Persian miniatures of ancient origin in a private collection in Kabul, possibly from Herat, possibly from Bokhara or elsewhere to the north. I saw no native art besides the primitive decorations on buses and some furniture. Likewise, there were virtually no professional musicians in the country, although by the time I left there had been some beginning attempts by Radio Kabul to train and engage local players of native instruments and western ones to record and play music for broadcast. Radios blared in most of the bazaars, and one did not have to be in Afghanistan more than a few weeks before becoming familiar with every tune offered. One, the Pushtunistan hymn, was played nightly; another short piece of music was played over and over every evening; I think it was a sort of bridge between news bulletins.

Western taped music was beginning to make inroads, but record players were rare, since the electricity supplied fluctuated so much that record speeds could not be kept consistent and the result was an unnerving wavering sound. In Mazar-I-Sharif the restaurant proprietor had a unique solution to this problem: he had hooked up his hand-cranked Victrola to regular electric speakers, with eerie results when he forgot to re-crank the mechanism. Only in the Khyber Restaurant did one hear western music regularly played, and there it was a random selection of undistinguished pop.

So there was Afghanistan: no resources, minimal industry, only subsistence crops, virtually nothing to export, virtually nothing to attract a tourist except for the land's raw beauty and the primitive nature of the country itself. What made it a crossroads was nothing more than geography. It was not a place where conquerors came to live but to control, and thus no conquerors have ever subdued it for long. The British came and left in the nineteenth century, not so much to rule Afghanistan as to keep the Russians from being there. The Russians came and left in the 20th century, not so much to rule Afghanistan as to keep American influence from hemming them in. Like Alexander, like Ghengis Khan, like Tamerlane (Timur-i-lang), they came, they destroyed, and they left. When they left, there was less remaining than when they came. It is a country that has been destroyed over and over again.

Yet the Afghans, who are not really a nation at all but just a collection of tribes who happen to live in this area, endure. It is their country, and they feel a great affection for it. If it were not for the ambitions of tribal chiefs among them, and neighbors who want to control their lands, they would have remained a small nation of subsistence farmers and nomadic traders. That is what most of them were when I lived there and, after the ravages of the last decade, that is about the best they can hope to be in the foreseeable future. Nothing changes very much in this land, and that is the way its inhabitants, for the most part, would like it to be. Anyone who has lived there has experienced life as it was, in fundamental ways, hundreds or thousands of years ago. It was one of the few places on the planet where one could experience that. For Americans, who have everything, it is an experience beyond price to live in a land where there is nothing except kind, hospitable people living an uncomplicated, self-contained existence.

Food

MANY AMERICANS RELIED ON THE U.S. COMMISSARY for their food, flown in from the U.S. or Europe, and when we were invited to American homes it was often to enjoy delicacies which we could not find in the bazaars. Yet Afghan cooking, though essentially simple, is on the whole healthful, tasteful, and deeply satisfying.

Afghan bread, called nan, is the best bread I have ever tasted. There are actually many different kinds of bread; each village has its own bakery or bakeries, and the bread made there depends on the kind of wheat available, the kind of oven the baker uses, and the particular traditions of that village. But the best, for my money, is the bread in Kabul. You may have eaten something called "nan" at an Indian restaurant, or even an Afghan one in the U.S., but what you would encounter in Kabul is something entirely different, something worth describing in some detail.

Nan is made from a large mass of gray, gritty dough, kneaded by hand into a long, snowshoe-like shape about eight inches wide and about two feet long. It is stretched over a sort of pillow which is then pushed down into and against the inside wall of a huge oven, where it adheres from the natural moisture in the dough. After a minute or so, the baker reaches into the oven with a long-handled fork and pulls it off the wall, piping hot, then places it on a wooden ramp leading out of the shop. The bread slides down to the waiting customer on the street, who usually has a towel or other cloth wrapping with which to pick up the hot bread and take it home. One has to eat nan within an hour or less of picking it up at the bakery in order to get the full flavor; there are no preservatives used, and the bread loses its tang and texture very quickly. One must also inspect the back of the loaf before eating, for pieces of charcoal from the inside of the oven often adhere to the surface.

The bread has very little leaven, so it is not at all like the white air-filled western loaf with which we are familiar. It is only about an inch thick, but it is neither hard nor crunchy, as one might expect unleavened bread to be. It is soft, chewy, and rich with a nut-like flavor. Frank and I often bought a loaf of bread after work to devour, slathered with butter or margarine, which we could buy in cans from Denmark or Holland. From time to time, my mother sent me "care packages" with peanut butter, and that made a meal in itself, washed down with a pot of piping hot tea from Ceylon.

Peanut butter was one foreign product that one would never find in any bazaar. Americans love peanut butter. We consume tons of it. Outside of our country, it is hardly known, except as a flavoring in Indonesian and some Chinese cuisine. Europeans see it as an exotic food, or as slightly disgusting, and one must admit that it looks disgusting to anyone unfamiliar with it. When Americans began to drop food packages to Afghans in October of 2001, peanut butter and jelly were included. I had to wonder whose idea that was. Possibly there is a powerful peanut butter lobby in Washington, and dumping packets of it all over the Hindu Kush seemed like a good way to ensure that our peanut crop would continue to be profitable. But the reaction of Afghans to having peanut butter rain down was bound to be similar to how Americans might feel if another country took chicken guts and mashed them up and dropped them as emergency food supplies for our hungriest people. Mashed chicken guts are probably as healthful as peanut butter, but we feed them to dogs, not to people. One of the early news reports after the food drops began told the story of a woman who had fed the peanut butter to her donkey.

Also easily purchased at a nearby shop were lamb kabobs, not the thick, juicy chunks of tender meat one might think of but small, stringy pieces of mutton, cooked on little slivers of steel which are scraps left over from the manufacture of stoves. The greasy kebabs were best when wrapped in nan, which absorbed most of the fat, and four or five skewers with a nan wrapping made a great dinner, although Afghans rarely ate them like that.

Afghan restaurants served huge dishes of white rice, cooked in fat so that it was slightly yellow, chewy, and a bit on the greasy side. Hidden in the middle of plate of such *pilau* would usually be a tiny piece of mutton. But when Afghans prepared their own food, especially for their elaborate picnics, the *pilau* was more carefully prepared. A favorite was kabeli *pilau*, seasoned with strips of carrots and raisins. Sometimes chicken, usually cut up or shredded rather than served as a whole roast, was also presented. Another choice dish on picnics were little meat or potato dumplings in yogurt, called aushak and boolani. There might also be side dishes of cucumbers, onions, potatoes, and succulent melon pieces for dessert. There were also some wonderful stews and goulashes, slowly cooked with tomatoes, onions, and flavored with various spices, of which ginger, cardamom, and allspice seemed most favored. This was the standard fare for dinners in Afghan homes also.

What was entirely missing, of course, was pork. As a strict Moslem country, there was not a single pig to be found. Once a shopkeeper beckoned to me with a lustful gleam in his eye, as if he was about to unveil to me, under the counter, some piece of particularly choice pornography. It turned out to be a can of spiced ham. "Gosht-e-hoog!" (pig meat), he whispered, certain I would jump at the chance to purchase such prized contraband.

Butcher shops with pre-cut meat or refrigeration did not exist. Meat was hung on hooks, and a request for a pound of meat resulted in the shopkeeper slicing off a chunk of whatever happened to be nearby. There was no such thing as butchering; there was just dead meat, hanging and fly blown, curing when the weather was cool and slowly rotting when it was hot. A few meat purveyors knew that there was part of a beef carcass which was more tender and therefore sought by foreigners, and so one could sometimes purchase a filet, at a premium price. This was called pusht-maags, which means "back brains." Even pusht-maags needed to be pounded thoroughly to make it eatable unless it was stewed or slowly pot-roasted. Beef was not raised on grain, so it was tough and stringy, and one had to assume that the cattle which ended up in butcher shops were simply family cows which had reached the ends of their useful lives. Mutton, raised on grass and much more prized as a meat, was generally more tender, but it still had the strong flavor and odor which characterizes any lamb raised beyond its youth.

Beef generally cost about eight cents a pound, lamb about twelve cents a pound, a bit pricey by Afghan standards but still an apparent bargain for westerners used to paying, then, at least a dollar a pound at home for even the poorest quality meat. Come to think of it, meat of such poor quality was not available at any price in the U.S., but day-long stewing and a variety of spices made even the toughest meat palatable, and none of us ever felt that we ate badly during our stay in Afghanistan. We ate as much as we liked, far more than we would have eaten at home, and because the meat was so lean, and because we ate no fried foods at all, most of us maintained more healthy weights than before or since.

On one occasion, my roommate Frank informed me that he had just seen a donkey carcass brought into the shop across the street, the one we patronized. Sure enough, when I went downstairs to see for myself, there was a haunch of gray, greasy meat hanging there, unlike anything I had seen in the shop before. "What is that meat?" I asked the owner. "Beef," he told me. "Isn't that donkey?" I countered. "Oh, no!" he assured me, but not very forcefully. I didn't want to argue with him, but after that I looked much more carefully at the color of the meat we purchased. Not that I think Afghans ever ate donkey meat, or, at least, did so intentionally. But that was the strangest looking "beef" I ever saw.

When I was in Mazar-i-Sharif and had at times to cook for myself, I found it difficult to make meat tender enough, but a greater problem was a practice of the butcher shops there. In Kabul, the meat was cut off the bone with a knife before being wrapped in paper for the purchaser. In Mazar, the meat was hacked at with a hatchet, which resulted in bone splinters being driven into the meat. After several instances of biting into bone splinters, often too small to detect and remove, I asked the butcher not to hack the meat that way but, instead, to cut it off for me. He looked at me as if I were insane, or possibly just trying to put one over on him. "I can't do that," he explained. "Everyone gets some meat and some bone. Otherwise it wouldn't be fair." He was quite right, of course; meat cost less in Mazar than in Kabul, and that was the reason. If he had cut the meat off the bone, he would have had to charge more money for it. That particular marketing ploy had not penetrated to the wilds of the north yet.

Chicken was bony and stringy. It was purchased alive and killed in the market place, far more expensive than mutton, but a good alternative for a main course. One could even find, on occasion, turkeys for sale. The name for turkey is "fil-morgh," which means "elephant chicken," an apt description for these birds, although they were scrawny by western standards.

Milk and milk products were available, but they were off limits for us. It was not just that milk was unpasteurized, which would have made it dangerous enough, but that it was often adulterated with water, and water was the most dangerous carrier of disease in the country. We could, and did, boil all our drinking water, and then let it settle (and regain some of its taste) in large tanks which every American had in their kitchens. But boiled milk is just boiled milk, not much good for anything. We sometimes found imported canned milk in the bazaars, and we could use that for baking.

Similarly, all uncooked vegetables were out of bounds. The soil in which they grew was polluted with water infected by human waste, and so salads were out of the question. Cucumbers were safe, as were cooked carrots, onions, potatoes, and so on, all of which we enjoyed.

One of the peculiarities of shopping in Kabul was discovering what was written on the small paper bag which a shopkeeper might give you to take home a pound of sugar, salt, or the like. Paper, like so much else, was in short supply, so recycling was a regular part of life in Afghanistan long before it became the thing to do in the U.S. Tire treads were recycled as soles for bazaar-made sandals, which explained why one found the marks of tire treads in the unlikeliest of places, such as on mountain trails or along narrow riverbeds. Paper bags were made for shopkeepers by gluing together any discarded sheets of paper that turned up. That meant that one might actually be handed one's purchase of, say, a half-pound of flour in a small cone-shaped paper bag which, on closer inspection, turned out to be a letter you or a good friend recently received and discarded after reading.

Nuts were safe, and these were also easy to find in the bazaars. There were no peanuts, and almonds were rare. Most of the shops which featured dry eatable goods had various kinds of chickpeas, but these were unappealing to our taste. We did, however, find that one could buy, wash, and roast what we believed were apricot seeds, called *khasta*. Apricot seeds contain some cyanide and can be dangerous if not prepared correctly. Maybe *khasta* didn't come from apricots at all, or, more likely, the way we were shown to prepare them, first using vegetable shortening to coat them, then salting them, and then roasting them in our oven, removed whatever was poisonous. One of the problems of being in our situation was the lack of source of reliable information about such matters. Since we didn't see Afghans keeling over after eating *khasta*, we figured we could chance it. They tasted very much like something halfway between an almond and a cashew, and they satisfied our desire for the kind of snacks, such as potato chips, pretzels, peanuts, and the like, which were absolutely unobtainable.

Our oven, incidentally, was a unique creation we had ordered from a local metal smith. We had him build a three-foot cubic box with double walls and a hole in the bottom where we could place a hot plate to heat the whole affair. Metal workers in the bazaars could make almost anything one might want, not with great craftsmanship, but cheaply and easily if given clear directions.

The homes of Peace Corps volunteers were generally heated by a unique system invented by an American stationed in Kabul. It was a cylinder about a yard in diameter and four feet high, with a smoke vent at the top and an inlet vent at the bottom. A large canister, open at the top, and with a round hole about four inches in diameter in the bottom, was built to fit snugly inside. One then took a large wooden dowel, four feet long, to fit in that bottom hole, inserted it, and packed sawdust tightly around it. The canister was placed in the stove, the wooden dowel carefully removed, and a piece of newspaper inserted in the resulting tunnel in the sawdust, after which the top of the stove would be covered. Lighting that paper through the bottom vent would ignite the sawdust, which would then burn slowly from the inside of the cylinder outward. On rare occasion, if the sawdust had not been tightly packed, a lump would fall into the hollow central channel and ignite, causing a small explosion that lifted the stove's lid a foot or two and dispersed burning ash around our apartment. Ordinarily it took about six to eight hours for the all sawdust to slowly burn, enough time for us to enjoy sitting in our living room in the evening and go to sleep well before our apartment cooled. By morning, of course, the rooms were freezing, but we could then use an electric heater for the brief period before we left for work.

One of the staples of our kitchen was vegetable fat, not only for khasta but for *pilau*, for rubbing on baking potatoes, for cakes, and actually as a part of many dishes. The Afghans generally used fat from the fat-tailed sheep, called *roghan*, for this purpose, but most westerners found this fat too oily and unpleasant, too redolent of that lamb smell and flavor which is associated with fatty and overage lamb. On rare occasion one could find Crisco, or some European equivalent, in local stores, but more often we purchased something called Dalda, which came from India or Pakistan. I think it was some kind of palm oil. It came in big yellow cans and, like so many other goods which were brought in by truck, it would suddenly appear in every shop in the bazaar, and then a week or two later it would disappear and possibly not be seen for months.

Since the border with Pakistan was closed during the first year and a half of our stay, imported goods, even from India, had to be trucked in from Iran, except for small amounts smuggled in. So one day, in one of the few shops which specialized in imported goods, one might find a case of Dutch chocolate, or tobacco, or several cans of Danish butter, or Lu cookies from France. Or Dalda. All the shops would have these, and then they would be gone and one might never find them again. So shopping became a regular adventure. One never knew exactly what one might find, or for how long it would be available. Or what shape it might really be in, after having traveled to Kabul over bone-shattering roads in ancient trucks. Sometimes a can of Danish butter, when opened, proved to have something inside which more resembled cheese. Sometimes a whole five-gallon can of Dalda had a yellow tinge and a musky odor that made it unpalatable.

There were no alcoholic spirits in the bazaar, even under the counter. Various embassies had ways of bringing in liquor for their citizens, but Peace Corps volunteers did not have access to these, so any indulgence had to take place at one of the many parties for foreigners to which we might be able to cadge an invitation. Afghans of affluence and status seemed to have secret liquor supplies, too, probably brought back from travels abroad. In some homes, we were treated to a beer made in Iran, also a Moslem nation but one liberalized under the Shah and therefore allowing liquor production and consumption in limited and slightly secret amounts. It was not very good beer, but it had a great name. This was when one of the more popular beers in America was Hamm's, "from the land of sky-blue waters." The Iranian beer, in unconscious parody, was called Sham's Beer.

There was one other Iranian product found in most American homes, with a memorable name. It was a detergent, and its name was the same as a similar American product, Ivory Snow. Except that the Iranian word for snow, and therefore for this familiar product, was "Barf." Time to do the laundry, we'd say; go down to the store and get a box of barf.

Entertainment

B Y 1962 AMERICAN MUSIC WAS KNOWN ALL OVER THE
world, although it had not yet invaded local
cultures to the degree which would occur over the next
two decades, as new technology (the Walkman-style tape
player) brought the infectious rhythms of rock. Still, over
fifty years of Broadway musicals and thirty years of
Hollywood musicals, transmitted by radio broadcasts and
records, had made the sound of American popular music
essentially omnipresent on every continent.

Not in Afghanistan, however. Radios blared in the bazaar; it was
considered polite to play one's radio as loud as possible in order to share
the music with everyone. To my ears almost all of the music sounded the
same, but that was not entirely because the music was unfamiliar. Radio
Kabul did not have a large selection of records from which to choose.
Much of the music was from India or Pakistan, but some was created
locally, with the radio station's encouragement. But the instruments were
never western ones; they were sitars, or similar plucked strings, with many
varieties of drums, often accompanying by singing in a high-pitched
register, whether the singer was a man or a woman.

This was two years before the Beatles, and one assumes that western rock music eventually made inroads, as it did across the globe. After the fundamentalist Taliban regime took over, music was banned completely, an oppression of the human spirit difficult to imagine and unmatched anywhere in recent history. The most reliable confirmation, in my mind, of the Northern Alliance's recapture of Mazar-I-Sharif was the report that radios were blaring music throughout the bazaars.

Short-wave radio brought in distant stations when the weather allowed, but the reception in this mountainous country was irregular and distorted. Sometimes one could hear music from Russian stations, but as those were usually located in central Asia, the music was much the same as what Radio Kabul played. On rare occasion we could pick up music from Austria, the BBC, or Voice of America broadcasts, but there was always too much static to enjoy listening to anything except news.

Given these circumstances, it was odd that there was actually a concert in Kabul in 1964 by the Duke Ellington Band. This was arranged by the U.S. State Department as part of a Cold War effort to demonstrate that Americans were not the savages portrayed by the Soviets but, instead, rich in a tradition of artistic achievement. The year before, we had actually seen the Joffrey Ballet perform in the one theater designed for such performances, out at the grounds where the national celebration of Jeshyn (of which more later) was held. The Joffrey performed a fairly simple program designed for people unfamiliar with ballet, and it went over reasonably well with its audience, consisting in equal measure of middle class Afghans and the foreign community. But the Duke was pretty much a flop with the former, and by the end of his program most Afghans had left, although the Europeans in the audience found the evening a rare treat. There was something distinctly odd about watching and hearing the Duke tell his audience, "We love you madly," with his distinctive phrasing, more than once, and observing the blank stares which even the English-speaking Afghans in the audience returned. It must have been the Duke's strangest and most frustrating concert. His may have been the finest traditional jazz ensemble in the world just then, but half of his audience had never heard a clarinet or trumpet before.

This was also the era when Americans, especially on college campuses, were listening to folk music. The Kingston Trio, The Weavers, and Peter, Paul and Mary had been at the top of the charts for several years, and dozens of other folk singers, old-timers like Pete Seeger and

Josh White, balladeers like Harry Belafonte and Joan Baez, and new talents like Odetta were concertizing regularly. I was one of the many who, with a rudimentary knowledge of guitar chords, had memorized enough arrangements to entertain at summer camp or with close friends. One other volunteer in my group, Jan Mueller, and I had brought our guitars to Kabul, aware that we thus appeared as stereotypical American youth but also informed that, given the lack of other entertainment in Kabul, we might enjoy providing our own to one other and to our tiny group. It was not long before we became invited to parties given by the foreign community, and before we left Afghanistan we had given concerts at the U.S. Information Agency, at the Kabul hotel on behalf of the Red Crescent Society (the Red Cross is too close to a Christian symbol to be adopted), and at other venues. We had established a small repertoire, and, at least in our own eyes, were damn good folk singers. Well, we were certainly the best folk singers in Afghanistan because we were the only ones.

There was one good movie theater in Kabul, the Park, with comfortable seats, a decent sound system, and projectors which did not break down, although the fluctuating electric current sometimes made scenes a bit dimmer than the producers had intended. They showed American films for the most part, sometimes with Dari subtitles, usually films only a year or two old. There were a couple of other movie theaters in the city, but they were crowded and uncomfortable and showed mostly old films from India and even older films from the U.S. "The Mountain Road" with Jimmy Stewart seemed to play at a theater down an alley from the Kabul Hotel on a regular basis for the entire two years I was there.

More recent films were shown every a week or two at the U.S. embassy and were attended primarily by the foreign community and a few of their Afghan friends. But after "Exodus" was shown there was a complaint from some embassies representing Islamic nations that considered the film pure Israeli propaganda, and after that it was necessary to have as special pass to attend films there. It was a reminder to all of us that even in a non-Arabic country, far from Israel and in no way connected with ongoing tensions of that region, religious fervor and a tradition of restricted freedom of speech affected everyone's lives. I was thinking of this in October of 2001 when I heard that a "Pokemon" film had been banned in some Moslem country because of the appearance of a symbol in it which resembled the Star of David. Only by living abroad can one appreciate fully that it is not food, or music, or comfort which Americans take for granted, but freedom of thought.

Another popular form of entertainment in the American community was playing charades. The Ambassador, John Steeves, liked charades, and Peace Corps volunteers were uninhibited when it came to such silliness, so we had a sneaking suspicion that we were often invited to the embassy because of our willingness to play the game. We were actually invited out a great deal during our first months in Kabul. Perhaps the American community pitied us a bit, since we could not live at the same standards as they, and thus friends made sure we could enjoy the delights of western food and drink which we might otherwise be denied. The Afghan II Peace Corps group and later groups appeared less circumspect, in our eyes, than we pioneers had been. We were shocked to find that some volunteers had actually crashed an embassy party. Eventually invitations fell off except from the few close friends we had made.

But by then we had already decided that our exposure to too many Americans from the embassy or AID staff was unsettling. Too many Americans fit a pattern the opposite of what the Peace Corps was intended to represent. Too many complained of poor pay when, given the cost of living, they could save far more than they could at home. Our stipend was $100 a month, plus rent and electricity; we could rarely spend half of it. Other Americans, earning several hundreds of dollars a month, spent much of it on imported goods at the commissary, not even realizing that most of the same goods were available in the bazaars at a fraction of the cost. Some even bought staples like salt and sugar at the commissary, which was pointless. Many bought imported American bread, which my fellow volunteer Bob Pearson called "goo-goo bread," instead of trying the local breads that were so much better than anything found at home. The embassy imported turkeys from the States for Thanksgiving, but we celebrated the holiday at Bob Steiner's house, with an adequate local bird, and the spirit of camaraderie we shared with his family made that evening one I remember to this day, long after I have forgotten the many aimless cocktail parties, replicating an American form of entertainment best left at home.

There were no places, or none that I ever learned of, where Afghans publicly congregated to hear music, or sing, and certainly not to drink or dance. I believe that within the compounds which sheltered Afghan families singing or instrumental music was an important part of entertainment. I have heard Afghans described by television documentaries as lovers of music, and while that may be an exaggeration, there must have been a place for music in social settings, or the Taliban would not have forbidden it.

Social dancing, I am sure, did not occur. Afghan marriages were arranged, and dating was not practiced. Men and women did not even walk together in public, although one heard that innocent trysts might occasionally occur in the public gardens, between the children of westernized Afghans. Men and boys, however, often walked hand-in-hand down the street, a practice commented upon by Americans, who found it just a bit shocking. This was before our own culture became more enlightened about homosexuality and feared even such innocent manifestations of affection as hand-holding between men in public. Attitudes towards sexuality are often the least possible to explain or to change by rational argument.

I mentioned earlier that there was one national holiday, Jeshyn, where public celebrations occurred. Some years there was a "big Jeshyn" something like an international fair, and some years there was only a "little Jeshyn." We were there for little Jeshyn, but we did not attend all the various events because there were always huge crowds of people, shoving and pushing, occasionally trampling one another when mounted policemen tried to impose a primitive form of crowd control. Policemen did not seem to have been trained for this task; they would wait around on the outskirts of crowds and, without warning, try to move them out of the way by riding their horses directly into the mobs. If one was in the wrong place at the wrong time, one simply was shoved to the ground and walked over unless one shoved back.

The best event we observed, on a large grassy field near the Jeshyn grounds, was called "tent-pegging." Mounted horsemen, colorfully attired, rode at full speed while carrying a ten-foot lance, attempting to spear a small wooden peg embedded in the ground. It took split-second accuracy and excellent horsemanship, and it also took typical Afghan bravery, since any carelessness resulted in a spill onto hard ground from a galloping horse. Given the lack of good and convenient medical treatment, injuries such as this could have serious consequences.

There were also exhibitions of the national sport, *Buzkashi*, although the best examples of this were to be found in the north, where the buzkashi grounds were of unlimited size and the numbers of riders much greater. *"Buzkashi"* means "goat-dragging," although a goat is no longer used. Goats were found to tear apart too easily under the strain of this violent activity. Instead, a beheaded calf is the object which horsemen try to grab, from their saddles, and drag past a goal marker. In Kabul, there seemed to be teams, but in the north it appeared to be more of a free-for-all. In Kabul there were, supposedly, rules; in the north, I could discern none.

Imagine a polo match with several dozen riders. Imagine that instead of driving a ball down a field with a mallet the riders are supposed to lean from their saddles and grab the leg of a dead calf, dragging it down the field. Imagine that once a rider has successfully gotten hold of the slippery, bloody carcass he has to run a gauntlet of horses being ridden into his while other riders try to reach down and grasp the calf by another leg, hitting him with their fists, or with whips. Imagine that, on occasion, two different riders have the calf by two different legs, and are trying to ride off in different directions, while other riders surround them and commit every kind of mayhem possible. That's buzkashi. It is not a gentlemanly sport. It is confusing, exciting, and very dangerous.

There is a sports stadium on the Jeshyn grounds, and we were invited to attend a ceremony of colorful drills by students there. These were not very different from the kind of display performed in Communist China, masses of students doing choreographed drills with flags and banners. There were also sports competitions, and these were preceded by an Olympic-style march of the athletes around the stadium. By the time our Afghan II and III Peace Corps contingents had arrived, we were able to put together a basketball team, and so I was able to observe and photograph, in the fall of 1963, a group of Americans, with the flag, proudly marching in the Jeshyn stadium.

Looking back at those photos today is a sad experience. The American flag could not be displayed in Kabul for years. Our embassy was closed and abandoned after the Russians invaded, then burned a few days after September 11. The Jeshyn stadium was still used for soccer games, but under the Taliban it was also used for the grimmest of ceremonies: public executions of adulterous women, by stoning, or by pushing stone walls onto them, or, in the case of blasphemers, running tanks over helpless prisoners.

I recall the close of Jeshyn, with the grounds all illuminated by electric lights, and with showers of fireworks. Kabul never looked more beautiful. At night, with all the lights flickering in the clear mountain sky, it seemed on the verge of becoming a beautiful city. Now the city is in ruins, and the Jeshyn Grounds hold memories of countless barbarities. Jeshyn was a celebration of national pride under a stable government, but such a government, let alone such a celebration, is now little more than a hope.

Enshalla

THE EXPRESSION *"ENSHALLA"* MAY NOT BE UNFAMILIAR. It was the most common expression used by Afghan speakers. More than a word, it is an attitude towards life which must be thoroughly understood in order to comprehend what life is like in Afghanistan and other Islamic countries where the modern world is still struggling to be born.

"Enshalla" literally means "as God wills," or "if God wills." But it is not equivalent to the English expression, "God willing." Americans who might say something will happen, "God willing," mean only that they hope it will happen. "God willing" is similar to knocking on wood. *"Enshalla"* is a reminder that man is not responsible for his fate, cannot really determine his fate, and should be resigned to whatever happens rather than become invested in trying to make things happen.

In the Afghan dialect of Farsi, or Dari, there is nothing quite like our future tense, because one cannot say something is going to happen in the future. One cannot really say, "Tomorrow I am going to Istalif," with the same meaning as English conveys. One can use the present tense, as in English, to imply future action; "Tomorrow I go to Istalif" means much the same in Dari as in English, that I have a plan to do something. But we would be more likely to say, in English, "Tomorrow I will go to Istalif," or "Tomorrow I am going to go to Istalif." The closest translation to these words, in Dari, is "Tomorrow I will probably go to Istalif." The uncertainty is embedded in the tense; future tense is always contains a suggestion of probability. It is built into the language because it is built into the outlook of the culture.

Similarly, there are two even more common Afghan expressions, *"Parwa nayss"* and *"Parwa nadera."* These mean, more or less, "It doesn't matter." My roommate Frank once returned from his job and exploded in frustration because a worker at his bus repair shop had insisted on lifting an engine with a hoist in a totally incorrect and dangerous manner, as a result of which the engine crashed to the floor, nearly injuring some people and causing a great deal of damage. The man responsible then looked at Frank and said, *"Parwa nadera."*

"It doesn't matter?!!!" Frank shouted at me. "What's the matter with these people? He almost killed me, and he says it doesn't matter?"

What the man was actually saying was, "Look, nothing terrible happened, so don't be disturbed, please, it's no big deal, there wasn't anything we could do about it, so why get all shook up about something which is, ultimately, in God's hands?"

For the vast majority of people who lived in Afghanistan then, and probably for most who live there now, there simply isn't anything they can do about anything. If war kills their families, or drought brings starvation, or bandits control them, or the crops fail, or children die from disease, those are just part of life. One cannot control these things, so becoming upset about them accomplishes nothing. *Parwa nayss...* it doesn't matter, because that's just how it is. *Enshalla*. It is God's will.

It is not a simple fatalism, but something stranger to western eyes. It is an understanding that trying to control everything, or much of anything, leads to a certain frustration. Of course, that frustration was always my own, not shared by the people around me. I remember when a certain religious holiday, or "Id" (pronounced "eeed") was approaching. Moslem religious holidays follow a lunar calendar, just as Jewish holidays do, but the Jews long ago decided to add a month every so often so that, although Rosh Hashanah and Yom Kippur jump around from week to week every year, they always occur in the fall because the extra month brings everything back in place, more or less. The Moslem calendar has no such extra month, so the holidays slowly progress, occurring about ten days earlier each year. That means that the holy month of *Ramazan* (called *Ramadan* in Arab countries), during which everyone fasts and refrains even from drinking water during daylight hours, is a minor inconvenience when it happens in winter but a major sacrifice during the summer, when the days are much longer and the heat is intense. All the other religious holidays move around the calendar in the same steady progression; state holidays follow the western calendar.

Not being familiar with all of the holidays, we had to keep alert to learn when they were upon us if we wanted to plan a vacation or holiday trip. On one such occasion, I had heard that Id-e-Korban was approaching, and I asked my students. "Is it this Thursday?" I inquired. "Will there be school on Thursday?"

"We don't know, teacher," they would say. "Maybe. Probably. *Enshalla.*"

"Are you coming to school Thursday?"

"Oh, yes, well, maybe not, I'm not sure. Maybe it is Id-e-Korban."

"How will you know it is Id-e-Korban?"

"It will be on the radio."

"But I can't understand your language on the radio. Doesn't everybody really know when it's going to be Id-e-Korban? Who decides that?"

"Well, I think it is decided when someone sees the new moon. It is a mullah who sees it first, in Mecca, and then they send messages to tell everyone that it is Id-e-Korban."

"What if it is cloudy in Mecca?"

"Then I think they wait until someone else sees the moon, maybe in Medina, or Jerusalem, or Baghdad. I don't know. It will be on the radio."

"Do you have a radio?"

"No, teacher."

"So, are you coming to school Thursday? Should I come?"

"Well, teacher, I think you should come, but it will probably be Id-e-Korban."

So, on Thursday, I went to school, and there were about a dozen students wandering about, doing nothing much. "It's Id-e-Korban, teacher," they said. "Why are you here?"

"Why are you here?" I asked. Some of them had bicycled for miles in the early morning frost to get there.

"Oh, I don't know. I just thought I'd come."

I was annoyed at having missed extra hours of sleep and comfort for no reason. But the students were happy and smiling and not in the least disappointed to have come to school on a holiday. After all, there wasn't much for them to do otherwise. One day was pretty much like another. It couldn't be helped. Why let such silly things annoy you, when it was still a nice day and nothing, really, had happened of any importance? *Parwa nayss.*

One of the greatest difficulties for all westerners in Afghanistan was trying to think in western terms of planning, objectives, steps to accomplish something, order, procedures, and all that was necessary to employ technology to achieve a given result when many of the people with whom one worked knew, deep in their hearts, that such an approach was pointless, since destiny was not in human control.

In the thirty-seven years since I left Afghanistan, I have lived a typical western life, planning goals and trying to achieve them, and succeeding more often than not. Thirty-seven years ago, Afghanistan seemed to be changing swiftly towards a western way of thinking; when I look back in my diaries from that era, I note my delight at the new buildings which were being erected and the political changes I saw occurring. In less than two years, I saw what I (and everyone else) thought was important progress for the country and the people living there. In 2001, I am chagrined to realize that the Afghan view of life proved more accurate than my own, that the future of my Afghan friends was in God's hands (whatever is meant by "God") and nothing I did, or anyone else did, during my two years there really made any difference at all.

Pay No Attention

THERE WERE SOME THINGS THAT ONE HAD TO CHOOSE not to witness. There were other things that I witnessed but had to ignore.

During our stay we heard of a public hanging scheduled in Kabul. Most of us had no desire to attend but, on the other hand, it seemed like a unique opportunity, part of a complete education, to observe such an event. If you were transported by time machine to the Middle Ages, retaining a modern sensibility, would you be careful to avoid public hangings and floggings and beheadings, or would you want to see and understand fully what medieval life was like? We were living in what was, in many ways, a medieval society, and a public hanging, it seemed, was part of that life.

As it turned out, we were advised by our Peace Corps mentors not to attend, whether we wanted to or not. The sensibilities of educated people in Kabul were such that they felt embarrassed by the existence of such barbarities in their land, and officials didn't want foreigners to witness them. It was advice easily followed. Yet knowing that the event did occur made it much easier to understand how it could be the case, forty years later under the brutal reign of the Taliban, that executions of adulterous women by stoning, or executions of others who had violated their edicts by even more horrible methods, had become common events.

It was impossible to avoid observing cruel treatment of animals, and it was not our role to interfere. Dogs are generally considered filthy creatures, and few if any of the dogs one saw in Kabul's streets belonged to anyone. They were miserable hungry mongrels, scavenging for a living, and shopkeepers felt no compunction about throwing rocks at them to drive them away. Bob Steiner told us of his experience years before in Iran, when a neighbor had a problem with servants who wanted to wash dishes or clothing in the swimming pool and would not refrain from doing so until they were assembled so they could observe the family dog swimming in the pool. After that the pool was considered unclean, unfit to function as a dishwasher.

Donkeys, the primary beast of burden, are mistreated in many lands. Afghans are not unique in beating these little beasts of burden when they fail to move at an expected pace or balk at moving at all. But I was not prepared to see the angry owner of a usually faithful beast which had decided to stop dead in the middle of the street resort to kicking it, determinedly, in the balls. I saw this more than once and wondered if animals so treated ever became enraged and turned on their owners. For an American to interfere to protect an Afghan donkey was entirely out of the question, sadly, so when we saw such things, we turned away or moved on, rather than be considered obnoxious foreign fools trying to disrupt a troubled businessman.

It was at school that I observed events that were impossible to ignore.

The first of these occurred one morning after I had been working at Lycee Nadiriya (a middle school in Kabul) for about six months. There had been problems with students arriving late, a problem I had hardly noticed, since an indifference to time was embedded deeply in the Afghan culture and the difficulty of finding reliable transportation anywhere was generally acknowledged. So it hardly seemed surprising, or significant, that many students regularly arrived late.

Apparently, however, the headmaster had been reprimanded by someone from the Ministry of Education, or for some other reason known only to him had decided that the problem had become one to be dealt with suddenly and firmly, which was why I began my first class one morning with an almost empty classroom, informed by the few students there that the other students were waiting to be disciplined at the

51

headmaster's office. And sure enough, I found a long line of boys waiting there, nearly half the students at the school, I estimated.

What they were waiting in line for was to be beaten on the hands. The headmaster had a large pile of green, freshly cut sticks, not branches but some sort of heavy reeds. Each student would enter the office and be told to extend an open palm, and the headmaster would then hit the student with full force across the hand with one of those reeds. The student would yell, and possibly tuck the beaten hand under his armpit, pleading for mercy. The headmaster would then tell him to extend the hand again, and the process would be repeated until the student was whimpering and begging to a satisfactory degree. Being brave and failing to cry out or plead for mercy was a hopeless tactic; each student was whipped until the requisite degree of pain, humiliation, and repentance was demonstrated. It did not seem to have anything to do with how often a student had been late, or how late he had been. It was, instead, a simple demonstration of the headmaster's power, intended to create fear, and it certainly succeeded in that regard.

I forced myself to watch for several minutes, but I could not tell my headmaster, who was supposed to be my boss, to stop. I expressed my discomfort by my expression, I am sure, but I did not feel it was my role to express my total disapproval by word or deed. When I returned to the classroom, however, my students picked up on my feelings without my having to say anything at all. It was obvious that I was very disturbed and unhappy. "Oh, teacher," they said. "You are very kind."

A year later, when I was teaching at a boarding school in Mazar-i-Sharif, I arrived one day to learn from my students that something very similar was about to happen. I was told that almost one hundred students had run away from school; holidays were only a day or two away, and they had decided to begin their holidays early. Those who could be apprehended had been found, dragged back to school, and were to be beaten. I suggested to other teachers that it might be better if I did not stay around the school that day, and they readily agreed. They knew that westerners did not approve of this kind of treatment of students, although I doubt that they knew about how similar treatment of students had been common in most western nations only a generation or two before. Paddling in schools in the U.S. is still legal in half of our states. I wonder how many adults would support this if they ever had to observe an actual occurrence.

It was back at Lycee Nadiriya, however, that I had my most disquieting encounter with violent behaviors. I was teaching my usual class one morning when there was a commotion in the courtyard which all the classrooms overlooked. One of the older students, probably around thirteen, was being pulled along by one of the menials who was responsible for sweeping the school, watching over the storerooms, and the like. The boy had his ankles tied together with a rope. When the flunky who was dragging him there arrived at the center of the courtyard, he tried to hold the boy, upside down, by the rope around his ankles and then beat the naked soles of his feet with one of those heavy green reeds he had brought. The ensuing struggle was long, loud, and brutal. The boy yelled and begged and thrashed around, often causing his tormentor to drop the rope so that the boy fell to the ground and could not be beaten, at which point the rope would be seized, the boy up-ended again, and the beating resumed.

I tried to look away and keep teaching, but that was impossible. The demonstration had been arranged so that all the students would see it, and the boy's howling could not be ignored. The students did not seem to be especially perturbed, however. "He is a very bad boy, teacher," they told me. They felt, apparently, that he deserved what he was getting, more or less.

"We do not hit people on the feet in my country," was all I could think of to say. It was obvious that I was dismayed, but I did not want to challenge the belief that malefactors deserved punishment and, since I didn't have any idea what the boy had done, I really couldn't explain why the punishment bothered me. For all I knew, it might have been deserved, but it still unnerved me to see someone beaten on the soles of his feet.

"Do people hit children in your country?" they asked.

"Yesss...," I admitted. "But not on the hands. Or the feet. They hit children... " I didn't know the right word. I pointed to my backside.

I think the students were more shocked by this admission than I was at the spectacle outside. There was a buzz of conversation, and some giggles, and some obvious embarrassment. Clearly, the area I was talking about was a forbidden area. It was a sexual area, as we all know it is indeed. Striking the buttocks would have been an act of extreme disrespect and, to a great extent, disgusting.

Suddenly, I felt that I was the barbarian.

Is This a Teacher?

I HAD TAUGHT FOR TWO YEARS BEFORE JOINING THE PEACE Corps. There were five of us altogether with similar backgrounds, teaching at four different schools, and our experiences in Afghanistan certainly taught us far more about our profession than anything we had encountered before, and probably since.

We were given extensive training in TEFL (Teaching English as a Foreign Language) during our eight-week stint at Georgetown. None of us had any background in that particular skill, so we welcomed all the training offered. It only took about three or four days on the job in Kabul to discover how incongruent much of that training was.

Our instructors were familiar with teaching foreign students in the United States to speak English. The major texts created for that purpose, by Lado and Fries, had been developed in connection with instructing Spanish-speaking students. We were soon to discover that a Spanish-speaking student in America has little or nothing in common with a Dari-speaking student in his own country.

To begin with, Afghanistan was a bilingual nation. Actually, it is a multi-lingual nation, but two languages predominated: Dari and Pushtu.

(Dari was not what the language was called when we were there; it was called Farsi, which is the language of Iran, but nationalism eventually required that Afghan Farsi have its own designation, and ever since then it has been called Dari.) Pushtuns live mostly in the south and southeast (as well as in Pakistan) but they have been the dominant tribe in the government for some time. Yet Pushtu is a difficult language for most Dari-speakers, and Dari is close enough to Farsi that it can share a literature and tradition which Pushtu lacks. Although the king and his family were Pushtuns, the court language was Dari, perhaps for some of the same reasons that the court language of the Russian monarchy was once French.

The government's decision had been to educate all Dari-speakers in Pushtu, and all Pushtu-speakers in Dari, beginning in third grade. So before they began learning English, our students had been through the experience of trying to learn a second language, generally taught by rote memorization, similar to the way languages were then taught in American schools, with similarly dismal results. Few Afghans were truly bilingual.

But there was another language Afghans had "learned," too, from the time they began school. The Koran is in Arabic, and the Koran is viewed by Islamic scholars as essentially untranslatable, since it is the word of God given to Mohammed, much as Orthodox Jews consider that the Torah should only be studied in Hebrew, the language in which God dictated it to Moses. Students were expected to learn the Koran in Arabic, which meant learning by pure rote to make the appropriate sounds without necessarily understanding them at all. Arabic teachers simply had students repeat words and sentences. They explained what these sentences meant. But there was no teaching of grammar or vocabulary as such, and no attempt to teach students how to read material they had not seen before.

Most of the Taliban were trained at schools in Pakistan, religious schools called *madrasas* where the only teaching is of this type. Films on American television show young boys (girls being excluded from schools in recent years) repeating phrases from the Koran, singing them loudly while bowing rhythmically, ironically resembling nothing so much as Orthodox Jews davening. They have learned Arabic words, and they have been told what those words mean, and that is the sum total of their education. They cannot question whether the mullahs who teach them actually know themselves what the words mean, and many of them do not. It is a pure oral tradition. Under these circumstances, the Koran itself has ceased to be a source of enlightenment, since it is not actually being "read" at all. All that is happening is the passing down of often misunderstood words without context, something like the game of "telephone" at an American child's party. The connection between what is learned and the original source of that learning has long since disappeared.

Granted, when we taught in Kabul, there were other forms of education besides this form of religious instruction, although much of it was not much better. A decade before, instruction at the best school in the city, Habibiya, had been excellent, since the staff had been almost entirely American, and many of the educated Afghans we met had learned not only English, which they had learned well, but other subjects at Habibiya. But as the government attempted to increase educational opportunities, it needed to open new schools; that meant quickly training new teachers, and the overall quality of teaching had declined. By the time students began to study English (or French, or German, depending on which school they were attending, although English was offered in most schools) they had experienced about six years of learning Arabic by rote and three years of learning their country's other language by traditional methods. That experience did not prepare them for what we were about to offer.

We had been trained in what is known as "pattern practice," repeating simple phrases with simple meanings, and then varying the phrases to bring out grammatical patterns, thus slowly building up these patterns of spoken English so they became habitual. It is the best method to teach a foreign language, and variations of it are used in almost all American schools today, although it was essentially unknown when I began teaching in 1959. But our Afghan students, confronted with this strange form of teaching, often looked at us as if we had lost our minds.

"This is a pencil," I would say, holding up a pencil. Then, in Dari, I would say, *"Een pensil ast."* I would then tell the students to repeat my words in English, and we were off and running. "Is this a pencil?" I would say, and then have them say. "Yes, it is. It is a pencil."

From there one would slowly build up a rich set of patterns, but not a huge vocabulary. Vocabulary can come later; first one has to master the structure of a language and be able to go off on such tangents as "The pencil is green. The pencil is not green. Give me the pencil. I give you the pencil. Do you want a pencil? I will give you the pencil. I did not give you the pencil." And so on. It sounds so easy, unless you really examine the baffling underpinnings of our language, where "It is. It is not. Is it?" is used side by side with "I give. I do not give. Do I give?" Two entirely different ways of forming questions and negatives, but English speakers do this instinctively. That's what we wanted our students to do, without thinking, and endless drill in these patterns was the quickest, if most boring, way.

Students were curious, of course, and often asked questions which I could not readily answer. Why do you say, "This is my pencil" instead of "This is the my pencil?" When do you say "a pencil" instead of "the pencil?" What is the need for using "the" at all? I had never really thought about the fact that, in my first lesson, I would say, "This is a pencil" and then, ever after, refer to that pencil as the pencil. It is obvious to us, but it has no equivalent in Dari. *"Een pensil ast"* simply means "This pencil is." If you want to say, "This pencil is green," the structure is the same: *"Een pensil sabz ast."*

We teachers compared notes and slogged on through pattern practice for weeks, feeling pretty good about being able to elicit what sounded like intelligent responses from our students to our endless queries about pencils. Of course, we were asking questions which had only one answer. It was a shock for each of us when the day came to try to go a step further. I vividly recall my interchange with the class that day, about three weeks after I began.

I held up a pencil. "Is this a pencil?"

"Yes, teacher," they chorused. And some brave students would add, "Yes, teacher, it is a pencil."

I held up a green pencil. "The pencil is green. Green... *sabz.*"

"The pencil is green."

"Is the pencil green?"

"The pencil is green."

"Is this a green pencil."

"Yes, this is a green pencil."

I held up a red pencil. "Is the pencil green?"

"Yes, teacher," they responded.

"No," I said, "the pencil is red. Red... *soorgh*"

"The pencil is red," they responded, confused but agreeable.

"Is the pencil green?" I asked.

Now I had created total confusion. "Yes, teacher. No, teacher. The pencil is green. It is red. It is not red." They tried any answer at all to appease me. "This is a red. This is not the green."

I had stepped over an invisible line of the Afghan elementary education system, and I would step over it often. I had expected students to use English to actually communicate instead of to parrot phrases, while everything in their background had taught them the opposite. When a teacher asked a question, there was a right answer, and that was whatever the teacher said it was. The answer had nothing to do with reality. You weren't supposed to try to figure out if the pencil was green or red; you were supposed to figure out what the teacher wanted you to say.

I should have had a clue from the art lessons I had observed. Art was taught one period every week. An aged man came into the classroom with a sketchpad. He would draw on the pad an outline of a bird, or a flower, or a chair. Then all the pupils would try to copy his drawing. They never looked at a bird, or a flower, or a chair. One was not trying to draw a bird, after all. One was trying to please the teacher, and certainly he knew what a drawing of a bird was supposed to look like, so that was what your drawing was supposed to look like.

I had spent weeks teaching the children to say whatever they thought I wanted them to say, without worrying about whether it meant anything at all. They were learning English the way they learned Arabic, as a bunch of sounds produced to please the teacher. Except for the rare students, the ones who asked me what "the" meant, and how to use it, they really didn't care at all what any of it meant. Foreign languages didn't mean anything, anyway, in their world.

I had to start all over again.

Yes It Is, No It Isn't

ONE OF THE TEACHERS FROM COLUMBIA TEACHERS' College, which had been a presence in Kabul for many years, reported hearing a young Afghan boy greet him in the street in this manner: "Is this a teacher? Yes, it is. No, it is not." I cannot vouch for the truth of the story, nor for the one about the young Afghan man, obviously somebody who had heard BBC broadcasts, addressing another foreign visitor by saying, "Good evening, listeners."

In spite of all the difficulties of teaching English, there were a remarkable number of students who learned well, learned quickly, and became highly competent. At the end of my first year of teaching at Lycee Nadirya, I gave a written test, and not an easy one, and I have kept a few samples in my files, both to encourage me when I recall all my failures and to bring me back to earth in case I abandon an appropriate degree of humility recalling my service in Kabul.

I included simple fill-ins, multiple-choice questions, and, throwing caution to the winds, questions to which the students were supposed to write actual answers. I had an Afghan write out instructions in Dari for me, and the students did seem to understand what they were supposed to do.

The results ran an amazing gamut. For example, one question asked students to use a word in a sentence. Here are some results from one paper; the word to be used is in parentheses, followed by the student's response:

(bad) It is a bad pen. [perfect]

(needs) He needs a pencil [perfect again]

(opening) I am opening the door. [wonder upon wonder... this, from a seventh grader, in his first year of learning English!]

Here is another:

(bad)   thm fo bab fofptl

(needs) bass a nob s yasuais

(opening) bas tahna bobank ys is

How does one account for this? How can one explain that one student, in response to the question (in English) "Do you like oranges?" writes "Yes, I do." with perfect capitals, and a period at the end of the sentence, and another writes "naaoymdo" (I think that second response was intended to be "I am do" meaning "I do," but that is just a stab in the dark.)

Not that the exam was especially useful in determining grades. Not that it was useful at all, except to force me to confront the amazing diversity of what had been occurring among the roughly forty children I had in each class. I had been trying to grade them on oral work all along, but with so many children, trying to give each a chance to recite every day was virtually impossible. Even more than in American classes, few of my students refrained from interrupting one another, answering questions not intended for them, feeding answers to the laggards, laughing at the totally inept, and engaging in every other behavior which bonded them together as a playful bunch of kids, rather than a class. Their Afghan teachers insisted on rigid discipline, which was not difficult to enforce when classes consisted of listening and repeating, or looking and copying, or reciting from memorized passages. As American teachers of language, we were doing the opposite of everything these students expected, and they must have often been completely bewildered by our odd behaviors.

Moreover, friendship is one of the preeminent values in Afghan society, possibly the most important value of all. Helping a fellow student by telling him the right answer is not cheating; it is a duty. At the same time, one does not show deference to other students if they are of a different tribe or a minority culture. Some students had no standing at all in their social group, and interrupting them or ridiculing them was nothing out of the ordinary. Looking back, I suspect that the poor student whose incoherent answers I recorded above was not simply dull, although he was that, but also a Hazara, which is a tribe that has no standing in Kabul, since they have Asian facial features and are limited, for the most part, to coolie standing. Some believe them to be descendants of Ghengis Khan's sojourn in Afghanistan, and others suspect they may be the original inhabitants, displaced by later invasions of Indo-Europeans, but in 1962 they were generally hewers of wood and toters of water, and they had to be unusually bright and assertive in order to make it on their own, without the support or respect of their classmates.

Another hindrance to the education of many of the students was their frequent absence. Some students didn't show up until the school term was three or four weeks under way. My Nadirya students were pretty good about showing up regularly, but some came from a good distance, and that meant they were often late. Some students were regularly called out of class for various duties around the school. And at my last school, Tejaraty, my now-disintegrating roll book shows that one-third of the class was absent for at least a week during the late spring. Classes were held, usually, about four times each six-day school week, so missing a day or two meant missing a lot.

Even when all my students were present, interruptions were to be expected. Various people came into the classroom intermittently to make announcements. Schedules were changed without much notice. Sometimes much of our meager classroom furniture, rough-sawn tables and benches, disappeared.

On one occasion I found three-quarters of my students standing when I arrived in class; all their benches had been taken away, I was told, by the school custodian, who had locked them up in the storeroom. Custodians in Afghanistan are held personally responsible for the furnishings they care for, and so when too many benches had become damaged the school custodian, having been reprimanded by the Headmaster, decided to lock up the furniture so it could not be damaged further. Faced with a class of standees, I went to the Headmaster's office and explained the situation, and he agreed with me that it was an untenable situation which he would see rectified. So the next day, when I arrived at the same classroom, my students were all seated, but arose to give me a standing ovation. They were most impressed by the power I had shown to have their needs attended to. And I basked in that admiration for the entire period. Then I went to my next class and found all the furniture removed; the school custodian had just switched it from one room to another to pacify us for a day.

As we advanced from oral to written English, we encountered new difficulties. Afghans use Arabic script, even though theirs is an Indo-European language. Dari is related more closely to English than to Arabic, both in structure and vocabulary, but the historic fact that it was Arabs who first spread Islam to Persia led to the adoption of Arabic script when Dari became a written language. Arabic script does not always put spaces between words; spaces are dictated by the specific letters used, with some letters coming to a full stop and others linking to the next letter in a word. The amount of space which we use between words in our script, and the amount of space we use between letters in the same word when we print, is culturally determined, something which seems so obvious that we do not notice it until someone used to an entirely different script, with different conventions about how letters are or are not spaced, writes in English. Every teacher of our group learned this dramatically with one of the first written lessons we used, where students were supposed to write, "My pen is on the table." As often as not, it came out, "My penis on the table."

Nevertheless, with all the stumbling blocks I encountered, I actually looked forward to that final exam as something which would provide me, I believed, with some concrete measure of what my students had accomplished during the year. We had done only oral work for the first half of the year, and my rough notes about what each student had learned were little more than educated guesses. I had not had time to test at all once writing instruction began; all I could do was glance at their notebooks from time to time and try to correct the most obvious problems.

So I spent a great deal of time creating exams which would test whether students really understood how to form sentences, how to change them from declarative to interrogative, from positive to negative, how to use plurals, and even how to read a series of short sentences and make sense of them. By the time my first teaching year had ended, the Peace Corps office had acquired a mimeograph machine and ample supplies of paper, so my students were about to become familiarized with those blurry, purple test sheets which were standard in American schools until modern copiers displaced them a few years after I returned to the U.S.

Nobody had told me that all final exams were given in the huge assembly hall, now filled both on and off its stage with the school's tables and benches, jammed together so that students, especially my students in the balcony, had to walk across table tops to take their seats or to leave them for bathroom breaks.

Nobody had told me that most final exams would be read aloud to students by their teachers, all over the room, so that my students had to hear those teachers shouting instructions during the hour they were trying to take my exam.

Nobody had advised me that students would cheat as much as they could, to help their friends. Since they were jammed together cheek by jowl in a noise-saturated room, with students climbing over the desk tops at irregular intervals, it took little skill for one student to tell another what to write, or for any student to see, at his elbow, what his classmate had written. It wasn't even a matter of the students engaging in subterfuge; they openly spoke to one other, looked at papers nearby or in the row in front of them, and simply did whatever it took to get down on those purple mimeo sheets whatever was likely to please me. It was chaos. I hadn't seen it coming, and I felt as if my whole year's work was spiraling down the drain before my eyes.

In the fullness of time, today, I don't think their cheating mattered at all. Whatever the future held for them, my little final exam was a tiny leaf in the wind. Some of those students are now adults living happy lives in the U.S. or other countries. Some of them are living miserable lives of poverty and desperation in Afghanistan or in a refugee camp across the border. Many are dead. Those futures were determined by circumstances which had little to do with me or my attempts to teach them English.

Still, I like to think my teaching did make a difference in a few cases. I actually met one of my students only a couple of years later, when he was an exchange student in the East Bay and looked me up. I didn't remember him clearly; I had taught hundreds of students, and their names had faded from memory rapidly. But this student had made it to the U.S., somehow, against all odds, to my complete surprise. It could not have been only his English skills that brought him here, either; he must have absorbed some of the feeling of what western schools were like, the freedom teachers and students have, and the respect they accord one another.

One cannot teach a language in isolation. One teaches an entire mind-set which the speakers of that language share. I'd like to believe, even though I cannot have any evidence, that more than one of those students in my classes learned not only how to speak or write English but how to think for themselves, how to see the world with different eyes, and how, as I needed to do, to liberate oneself from the strait-jacket of one's own culture.

▼▼▼▼▼▼

Zenda-ba-Non

MY ROOMMATE, FRANK BRECHIN, WAS THE ONLY mechanic in our group, so his perspective on Afghanistan was unique. More than the nurses, and far more than the teachers, he was dealing daily with the problems of labor in a technical field within a culture which not only had limited technological experience and know-how but where traditional values clashed with the infrastructure necessary to adopt modern technologies.

Zenda-ba-Non was the major automotive workshop in Kabul, servicing private and government vehicles including about 300 buses, both Soviet and American. It was one of the largest such workshops in Asia and had been supplied with ample tools and machinery, primarily from AID. But the tools were hard to get into the hands of the workmen. From fear of theft, tools were kept in a storeroom and had to be requisitioned one by one when needed, even nuts and bolts, even rags. Just as it was with books and furniture at the schools where I worked, the storeroom custodian was expected to pay out of his own pocket for anything which was missing, and so it became his major role in life to prevent anything from being taken out of the storeroom.

Day after day, Frank would come home after work and say to me, "You won't believe what they did today." Most of the time he would tell me about how some tool was needed, and how he went to the storeroom to get it for one of the workers (since their request would be routinely denied) and he would be told it could not be found. Frank would ask to be let in to look for the tool, but to do this he needed special permission from someone high up in the chain of command, usually the company vice-president. So Frank would go find this person, not always an easy process, and get written permission to enter the storeroom, and then he would find the tool, but in order to requisition that tool after it was found, he often then had to go back to the same superior and get written permission to take the tool out onto the shop floor so it could actually be used. It did not help matters that the man in charge of the storeroom, who often had to locate tiny parts, was nearly blind.

The workers were generally poor, untrained, unskilled laborers who simply did what they thought might be adequate. They carried engine blocks on their backs from place to place. They held steel to be welded in their hands, shifting their feet to avoid hot metal sparks. When it came to tightening screws and bolts on engines, lacking the necessary tools, they did the best they could in a slapdash manner in spite of the possible consequences of connections coming apart on moving vehicles.

At first Frank worked in a bus assembly shop, but it was when he moved to the maintenance shop that he was able to do his best, if most frustrating, work. One of his chief frustrations was that private customers had ideas about their cars that were not based on anything other than asserting their own authority. One frequent request was to have the engine sprayed with kerosene to make it look shiny. Another was to forbid anyone putting water in the battery, fearing it would freeze. Frank got around the latter problem by telling customers that the water he was adding was acid. But the engine spraying, which was sure to cause rotting of rubber parts like hoses and belts, was just too painful for Frank to allow. He usually refused to do it, so some of the customers simply prevailed upon other, more easily intimidated workers to do it when Frank wasn't looking. In one case a customer of some status, who was used to getting his way, went to Frank's Afghan boss and insisted that Frank spray his engine as he wished. The boss came and ordered Frank's workers to do it, and, Frank told me, "the guy stood there and laughed at me as his engine was sprayed and its parts began to rot."

On the one hand, what Frank was accomplishing was the most critical work our volunteers were asked to do. There was more than adequate American technical assistance, but without daily observation of the details of how jobs were being performed, most of the materials were misused or wasted. Americans who supplied help with management could only do so much; without somebody seeing how that management was carried out, old work habits were the rule, and that meant habits acquired by people who had never used a tool more complex than a hammer or a saw. On the other hand, sometimes problems were ignored while awaiting the arrival of some new superior American product, which might take weeks or months, even though materials to solve the problem were already at hand. Frank was there to solve problems instead of relying on the will of Allah to make things right. But he paid a high emotional price.

One afternoon he came home deeply saddened. It seemed that a car had left the shop with a grease spot on it, and the owner was annoyed enough, and had enough clout, so that Frank's boss felt it incumbent to take some sort of action. He told Frank he had decided to dock two of the men who worked for Frank three days' pay. That was only about $1.60, but for someone earning $16 a month it was a substantial penalty. And it was an entirely undeserved penalty because, as Frank pointed out, those men were not responsible. The responsibility lay with a young boy, a trainee who worked without pay. Frank's superior told Frank he knew this but, since the trainee had no pay to dock, he had to dock the salaries of men who did. Frank pleaded. He reminded his boss that there were no rags to clean up grease spots except in the storeroom, and that those rags were never released without a special letter from the company's vice-president. The boy couldn't possibly have requested or received such a letter. Frank's pleading made no difference. The men lost their pay.

On another day, Frank sought permission to get three trouble lights on extension cords from the storeroom to hang under a car's hood while servicing it. The natural light was no longer adequate now that the winter months were approaching. Frank was able to locate the trouble lights and take them from the storeroom, but there were no bulbs in them. It took two more days to get a new requisition from the company vice-president for the bulbs, but then, it turned out, the bulbs he was given did not fit the sockets in those lights. This time Frank simply lost all composure; he marched into the storeroom, over the protests of the man who guarded it, and found the correct bulbs. Triumphantly, he screwed them into the sockets and plugged the cords in. Nothing happened, except for some amused looks on the faces of the workers there. There were plugs in the shop, but the electricity had never been hooked up. Those plugs had always been dead. Nobody had bothered to mention it to Frank, because who knew when electricity might flow? That was in the hands of God.

I don't remember exactly what it was which sent Frank in search of the company's elusive vice-president on the day when Frank came back to our apartment, lay flat on his back on the floor, and simply stared at the ceiling in stupefied bewilderment. There had been a minor crisis in the shop, one of those things that required the vice-president's approval in order to unclog a complete bottleneck. As usual, Frank was the only person who could approach this administrator who had achieved a high enough rank so that no one else could make important decisions such as allowing a screwdriver to be set free from the storeroom. Frank went to find him, but he was not in his office, and no one knew where he might be. Zenda-ba-non was not a small operation; Frank supervised 20 men out of a total of about 750. Finding the vice-president so he could allow work to proceed became a frustrating nightmare. He didn't seem to be in any of the places where Frank was directed, although everyone knew he had to be around.

But he was finally located. Zenda-ba-non, inexplicably, had decided it could make some extra money by storing walnuts in one of its maintenance yards. Four laborers had just delivered a truckload of walnuts, and they were counting them into bags. One worker would hold a bag, and another would count handfuls of walnuts into the bag. The vice-president, in charge of one of the largest auto shops in the world, was sitting on a stool, with two men to his right and two men to his left counting walnuts into bags. He was observing them to see that the count was honest. Hundreds of workers and many thousands of dollars of equipment were temporarily idled from fear that a few cents worth of walnuts might be stolen.

Frank ended his assignment at Zenda-ba-non in June of 1964 after about 21 months. The Afghan government did not request a replacement, and, as was observed in a report from American Field Service four months later, the changes in operation which Frank instituted began to fade away rapidly. It needs more than two years to change entrenched attitudes; sadly, without such fundamental attitudinal change, efficient technology cannot take hold. The travels throughout the country which I describe elsewhere were delayed by bad roads and bad weather, but they were mostly delayed by mechanical breakdowns so common as to be expected every two or three hours on the road. And those breakdowns were repaired on the spot by drivers without any of the means, the tools, or the small degree of experience which one could find at Zenda-ba-non, inadequate as it was. Afghanistan's transportation systems, for that reason, ran on hope and Band-Aid repairs.

There is one last story I have to tell, even though it may be apocryphal. It was told and retold by foreign staffers working in the country in the 1960s, and it has a ring of truth, even if the details may not be entirely correct.

It seems that there was a large warehouse which was visited by a new American AID representative, a storage facility filled with all kinds of American machinery and goods. But all these crates of valuable equipment were being carried about by hand, or sometimes by man-powered handtrucks. Much was mishandled and dropped, and items tended to be stored, willy-nilly, here and there, the place usually determined by the weight of the packing crate, heavy items being carried the shortest distance and light ones the furthest.

"What you need is a fork-lift truck," the American stated, explaining how this particular piece of equipment worked. "It would do away with all this wasted motion and damage. It would allow you to store things in an orderly fashion. It would be a wonderful piece of equipment for this place. I'll see if I can get one shipped out here."

And in a few months a crated fork lift truck made it across the ocean and across Iran and along the rutted roads of Afghanistan to Kabul. The American AID representative was there to see it uncrated and proudly to demonstrate how magnificently it was about to change everything. He showed one of the workers how to move crates around the warehouse, stack and unstack them, and generally bring order out of chaos. It was an impressive demonstration.

"How large a crate can it move?" one of the workers there wanted to know.

"Oh, any of these, easily."

"What about that really big one over there?"

"Certainly," said the American, and then demonstrated how easy it was to move the specified crate. It was, indeed, a very heavy, unmarked crate, but it was moved without difficulty. "What's in that crate, anyway?" the American asked.

"We don't really know," said the workers. "It's been here for quite some time, but we are not sure who sent it or why, so we have been waiting for directions about what to do with it."

You do see the end of this story coming, don't you?

Out of curiosity, they opened the crate. It contained a forklift.

Masdurat

THERE WERE THREE NURSES IN OUR SMALL GROUP, one of whom had more work experience than any of the rest of us. At 36, she had spent ten years more in her profession than her fellow volunteers, all in their twenties. The other two nurses were in the first or second years of their careers, but all three had an immediate impact, plunging in after only a few days at Masdurat Hospital for women, while the teachers found themselves waiting to fill what turned out to be only temporary positions a few months before the school year was about to end.

Like Frank, the nurses soon encountered frustrations with the lack of technical knowhow and adequate materials, yet like the teachers, they found equally frustrating a profound difference in cultural attitudes.

When it came to equipment, the problems were mostly those one would expect to find in a developing country. One thermometer was routinely taken from patient to patient after only a quick, ineffectual rinse in alcohol. Surgeons used gloves borrowed from nurses, no matter how many patients those nurses had attended or what diseases they might have. Anesthetic was not available for deliveries. One refrigerator in the whole hospital had to hold everything, and did, from blood samples to stew.

There was virtually no blood for transfusion, so patients anticipating surgery gave blood for themselves one week ahead of time to be stored and used if needed. Surgeries had to be planned well in advance anyway, because a chronic shortage of beds meant that even procedures that should not have been delayed, such as for a slipped disk or gall bladder infection, would regularly have to wait a month for attention.

Since the hospital did not have a functioning hot water system, hygiene was hopeless. Unscreened windows meant a profusion of flies everywhere. Isolation of patients with tuberculosis, common in the Afghan population, was not attempted. Even patients with meningitis could not be isolated effectively. Much of this sounds like a litany of sad but all too common problems found at clinics in rural Africa or Asia even today, but remember, this was one of the best hospitals in the most advanced city in the country. Of course, it was a women's hospital, and that may have explained some of the general indifference to conditions there.

Still, there were some problems which were uniquely exacerbated by Afghan cultural patterns. Our Peace Corps nurses were always complaining to the hospital about the lack of towels; ordinarily, two or three would have to serve for an entire ward. Meanwhile hundreds of unused towels lay locked in the hospital basement. Once again, the practice of making the guardian of the storeroom financially responsible for its contents resulted in those contents being locked away, unused but never lost or damaged, the only satisfactory outcome for the custodian, but a self-defeating practice. I never learned how many medicines, vaccines, bandages, and other crucial supplies lay rotting in that same hospital basement, but it is an entirely reasonable assumption that much of what was supplied, generally through American aid, was fated to remain unused.

There were, for some reason, a number of oversize towels in storage. One of our nurses tried to get permission to cut these in two; they were much too large for ordinary use but could help supplement the inadequate supply of regular toweling. The suggestion could not be acted upon. Records showed that so many towels of such a size were in the hospital's list of supplies, and so exactly that number of towels of that size would have to remain in the supply room. Even if they were useless, it was the practice to protect these imported goods, seen as unusually valuable, rather than to make them useful.

Our nurses also had to stand by and observe some medical practices contrary to their training. In one example, a dead fetus was removed by cesarean section when all indications were that it would have spontaneously aborted. In a case of osteomylitis, a tibia was removed as a substitute for amputation. Nurses may disagree with doctors from time to time in all hospitals, but our nurses found it especially difficult to keep quiet and ignore what was, from all their training, unacceptable medical practice. The fact that there were nurses in Afghanistan at all, women able to work alongside men, was a relatively new development, but they were still years from achieving power to make decisions.

For the five years of Taliban rule, women could not work at all in Afghanistan. During the period we were there, in spite of the frustrations noted above, women were making steady and dramatic progress. Many still wore the chadri, but it was not required; it would have been impossible for women to perform work at all so attired. Even non-working women, shopping in the bazaars, could appear with their faces uncovered, although their dress remained modest, with long sleeves, long skirts, high stockings, and scarves all but universal. Women were seen more and more often in offices around Kabul, and later, when a communist regime was in charge of the country during the 1980s, government positions were open to women at high levels.

One of the tragic ironies of the return under the Taliban to centuries-old attitudes was that not only were women deprived of medical services from male doctors, but men and boys became deprived of the services of talented, fully capable women doctors and nurses. Wounded soldiers undoubtedly suffered and died pointlessly as a direct result of the low level of care that had to result from such blind, pointless theology.

Not that all or even most of the Afghan nurses were highly trained. Nor were they efficiently used; even our own American nurses generally could not work for the first forty-five minutes of their shifts because everything was locked up and the people responsible for unlocking supplies arrived late. Once again, the Afghan lack of concern with timeliness was a barrier which westerners could find no way to overcome. Night nurses often failed to show up at all. So children of patients had to serve as their nurses, even during the day, which they did as well as could be expected.

With so many obstacles to a transformation from ancient to modern ways, the best one could do was to compromise. In one instance, a dead baby was found wrapped in paper in a linen closet. This looked at first like an attempt to hide a socially unacceptable birth through infanticide, but it developed that entirely different forces were at work. The baby had been delivered dead, and the doctor in charge believed that the death was due to an unusual, unfamiliar condition, something which needed to be studied to discover the cause of death and prevent similar cases in the future. Such study would best be undertaken at the medical school, in the best tradition of modern medicine. But there was no facility at the hospital to preserve the poor little corpse, and so the nurse who was handed the tiny body didn't know what to do with it. The best she could think of was to wrap the baby in paper and put it on a shelf, and so that is what she did.

My own personal contact with the medical establishment was limited to teaching some special courses at Kabul Medical School, part of the University. It was an assignment I undertook with some trepidation. Someone in one of the government ministries had heard that Peace Corps volunteers would undertake projects without all of the red tape which surrounded requests to and responses from other U.S. government agencies. Workers from AID were professionals in their fields and were not going to try something for which they were not trained and which would be unlikely to be accomplished with success. Failure to perform a job satisfactorily could be a bad career move. Most of us were not professionals of any standing, only volunteers; we had nothing much to lose by pitching in and doing the best we could. Probably we liked to think we were like our pioneer forefathers, tackling the wilderness in the days when American know-how was assumed.

Volunteer willingness to undertake tasks avoided by more experienced Americans sometimes led to problems. Ministries in developing countries often saw their status enhanced by having Americans working for them, so one of the complaints of early Peace Corps evaluators from Washington was that many countries had requested volunteers who did not have very much to do once they arrived in the host country. This was not a problem in Afghanistan, however; our evaluators found that we had plenty to do.

The specific request I was asked to respond to was to teach English medical terms to Afghan doctors who did not speak English. Texts which they needed to study abounded in English terms, since much of the major advances in medicine were made in English-speaking nations or reported in English language journals. These doctors needed English words, not English sentences. My training as an English teacher had emphasized that learning a language was learning its structure, not its vocabulary. Vocabulary without a pattern in which to fit it has no function at all.

What I had failed to account for was the tradition of Koranic teaching, a tradition which influenced all the learning going on in the country. Learning words and their meanings without necessarily putting them in any meaningful context was old hat to these students. They could do it quickly and easily, or they never would have been able to achieve enough status, within their own educational system, to enter medical school. I just had to figure out how to help them understand some of the terms from a list of translations which was supplied to me, and to explain (in Dari) how Americans used these terms, and clarify some of the subtleties of the vocabulary. That my knowledge of medicine was trivial, that my skill in speaking Dari was primitive, and that my training in this form of teaching was non-existent turned out not to matter. I puzzled out a form of curriculum, had some lists written up, met with the medical students several times in informal discussion, and after a few weeks, they seemed entirely satisfied that I had performed a valuable service. I was never certain that I had done anything at all, and my notes from that course at Kabul University are nearly incomprehensible to me today. But something happened, and we all felt good about it, whatever it was.

My sojourn at Kabul University also provided me with a macabre experience I still recall vividly. I was given a tour of the medical school, a fairly modern and efficient-looking place, as far as I could tell. What did I know? It looked clean and well-lit, more so than the middle schools and high schools where I had taught, and the students seemed to be eager and apt. The staff displayed evident pride in their facility.

Then we went into the basement. I wasn't sure what it was that they were about to show me when we approached what seemed to be a rectangular black steel tank in a rather dark room where the smell of formaldehyde was unmistakable. Then one of the menials who worked down there in the depths of the building took a long metal pole and pried up something from the liquid in that tank. It was a corpse. This was where they kept the cadavers for dissection. But, it appeared, they kept them there for a long, long time. And whatever the preservative they used might have been, it was not entirely effective. The rigid, gray body was covered with green slime. It looked like something out of a cheap horror movie.

I didn't really know what I was supposed to say. "Very nice," seemed out of place. "Yecch!" would not have been understood. So I said what Afghans often say when confronted by something which they are not prepared to deal with.

"Ah, yes," I said, in Dari. "I understand, sir. Very good."

Travel at the Speed of a Camel

I N ORDER TO UNDERSTAND AFGHANISTAN TODAY, ONE must realize that, although it is a nation no larger than Texas, it is separated into disparate tribes, languages, and regions, so that it is a nation in name more than in fact. Whereas the United States is comparatively huge, it has been physically unified, since the completion of the transcontinental railway in 1869, in a way that Afghanistan has never been.

Actually, the geography of Afghanistan makes any unity of the country problematic, and for most of history it has not been one country at all. The Hindu Kush, a range of towering peaks in the center of the country, forms a barrier between the north and south which effectively divides the land even today. Only because these mountains do not extend into the western parts of Afghanistan, where the land is mostly desert, have armies been able to invade the land from the west by travelling the long distances around the mountains and across that desert rather than forcing the passes of the Hindu Kush.

During my stay in Afghanistan, there were several occasions when I needed to or chose to travel. My experiences, and those of my fellow volunteers, were exercises in frustration in every instance.

To begin with, there was (and, I am sure, still is) nothing like a national transportation system. The closest thing to that when I was there, was Ariana Airlines, familiarly referred to as *Enshalla* ("if God wills") Airlines. Our initial entry to the country from Teheran was delayed three days because of some unspecified problems with one of the airlines' two jets. On three other occasions when I tried to make use of the airline (for reasons which will become apparent), I had to wait over two weeks for a combination of dry and warm weather, flight schedules, and equipment availability to catch flights to or from Mazar-i-Sharif. More of this in another chapter.

So transportation, unless one could hitch a ride with a friend, had to be by bus, and a bus trip in Afghanistan was a unique experience. There was one bus company that ran a regular scheduled service between some of the major Afghan cities, but one needed to make reservations in advance. Otherwise, each bus was privately owned, and so its destination, and the time of its departure, were of the owner's choosing.

There were no such things as bus stations, but there were parts of town from which buses departed, so one would go there and hear drivers shouting out where they intended to go. "Maimana... Maimana... Maimana... *borrrroooo!*" (Maimana, Maimana, Maimana, let's go!), you would hear. If and when enough people wanted to go to Maimana, they would climb aboard and leave.

The first trip Frank and I decided to venture upon, a weekend jaunt about 70 miles south of Kabul to Ghazni and back, was fairly typical. More than one driver was going to Ghazni that day, so more than one driver was encouraging passengers to join him. Potential riders would mill around, trying to figure out which bus would leave first. Frank and I made the mistake of getting on a bus that was supposed to go there and sitting down. We sat there for quite some time, watching others tentatively getting on and then getting off again until we figured out that we were doing something wrong. At that point we joined the mob swarming around several buses, and eventually, somehow, that mob decided they liked one bus best, and all of us suddenly jammed into that bus, and the bus left.

After a bus leaves it does not necessarily go very far. More often than not, a bus that was sitting waiting for passengers for many hours will, after traveling for a few minutes, stop and have the gas tanks filled. No point in filling the tanks until you really know you are going. It's God's will that you eventually go at all, so until that will is ascertained, why spend the money on fuel?

Then, of course, there are people standing on the street, or on the road, who want to get on the bus too. It is not possible to be inhospitable in Afghanistan, so anyone who wants to get on the bus can do so, no matter how many people are already inside. In fact, at a certain point, new passengers did literally get "on" the bus, rather than in it. They rode on the roof, on top of the luggage, which consisted mostly of bedrolls.

Afghans do not generally use chairs, unless they have been westernized. The normal sitting position is a squat; Afghans can squat very comfortably for any length of time, to chat, to eat, to drink tea, and generally to socialize. So Afghan buses, although the bodies come from abroad (International, known as "Eenternash," was the favored chassis), ordinarily had their interiors altered. The regular seats were removed and replaced with wooden benches about four inches from the floor. These are reasonably comfortable if one is used to squatting, but if you are used to sitting in a chair, you will develop shooting pains in your legs, thighs, and back sitting on these after about ten minutes in a bouncing, rocking bus. So, after the fourth or fifth unscheduled stop, Frank and I decided to generously cede our places inside the vehicle and go sit on the roof, where we clutched on as the bus swayed but found ourselves far more comfortable, with a truly excellent view of the countryside. So it was, sunburned but not exhausted, that we eventually arrived at Ghazni. It took about five hours to get there. Fifteen miles an hour was less than normal speed for an Afghan bus, but given the many stops and interruptions picking up passengers and performing repairs, this was normal progress.

That was the easy half of the trip.

The next day we had to return to Kabul, since travel had to be approved by some ministry which permitted such things, and we did not have proper papers to allow us to be away from Kabul for more than two days. Having seen the sights of Ghazni, we determined to make sure we made it back to Kabul in time, so we decided to find out where the departure area for buses was before we did anything else that day. We hoped to take a different route, through the city of Gardez, and buses for Gardez left from another departure area. We eventually found that spot and were repeatedly reassured that there would be a bus along "in half an hour." After several hours, we understood that the hospitable Afghans were simply telling us what they thought we might want to hear, rather than explain that no bus was likely to be available. So we walked back across town to where our bus from Kabul had arrived, but there were no buses there either. It was a holiday, and buses weren't operating.

We returned to our hotel (that's what it was called, but it was a simple rest house with several rooms of cots for our sleeping bags) and asked for advice. How could we get back to Kabul that day? Nobody had any idea. Wasn't there a bus? Oh, no buses? Well, maybe there would be one. Well, there would probably be a bus tomorrow. *Enshalla.* Why not stay in Ghazni? Oh, you don't have the right kind of permission. Well. Maybe something will happen. Don't worry. Everything will be good. *Enshalla.*

This was our first experience outside Kabul, on our own, and we suddenly felt a certain degree of panic. The last thing we wanted to do was to bring down the wrath of the government because two stupid foreigners hadn't followed regulations. We spent a lot of time wandering around, and having tea, and hoping that, *enshalla*, something would happen.

And eventually it did. We spied a row of trucks by a gas station, and one of the drivers offered to let us ride with him to Kabul when he left "at one o'clock." At one-thirty he made motions as if he was about to leave, and we started to get on his truck, only to be stopped by a soldier. The truck was part of a military convoy, and it wasn't going to leave just then anyway. Eventually we found an important-looking officer who gave us permission to ride with the convoy when it left "at four o'clock." At five-thirty, when it did leave, we were on it, along with an English tourist. One minute later, all the trucks stopped, and I got off to see what was happening. Our driver started his truck but told us not to get back on, as he was only pulling up a few feet. Then he drove off.

We flagged another truck and were allowed on, and after an hour and a half the convoy stopped again. We decided to look for our original driver to ask why he had abandoned us, but we couldn't find him. We did find the officer who had first allowed us on the convoy, but he now insisted that we could not continue, since it was a military convoy (even though there was nothing faintly resembling a war going on at that time, in Afghanistan or anywhere within a thousand miles). At this point we lost most of our composure. We were now in the middle of nowhere, we pointed out. We had no idea where we were or how to get where we were going. We could not get back to Ghazni. We were not birds who could fly. We would die of exposure, we explained. Bandits would attack and kill us. This last was not really such a far-fetched idea, and it may have been the reason that eventually the instinctive Afghan hospitality overcame prudence and the Englishman and I were allowed to get up in the front seat of a different truck at the rear of the convoy. I am not sure where Frank ended up.

The rear of the convoy, however, kept changing as one truck or another broke down and had to wait for repairs. It turned out that military convoys traveled even slower than buses. We seemed to stop every five or ten minutes for one reason or another, sometimes for long spans of time. Progress was glacial.

At nine thirty our truck stalled for the fourth time, and it began to rain. As we sat there, the entire convoy passed us by. We waited for a while, and then our driver went out into the dark to look around. He disappeared. At ten-fifteen my English companion decided to go to sleep, since we seemed to have been stranded. Around eleven, someone appeared and woke us; there was a village not far away, and we were invited into a teahouse to warm up. I think our driver had been there all along and suddenly remembered that hospitality demanded we not be left alone forever.

Around midnight, some other trucks from the convoy appeared out of the dark and helped our vehicle get started again, and off we went on a badly rain-damaged road. We stalled again for half an hour at two-thirty. Then, fifteen minutes later, we caught up with the rest of the convoy, and stopped again, this time for good. There was a washout from some kind of flash flood; what had been a bridge of sorts was a pile of scattered boulders and mud in a stream bed, and the trucks could not proceed.

About five, as the sun rose, we all went out to see more clearly what the problem was. We were on the outskirts of Kabul, probably about five miles away. So we all pitched in and started struggling to rebuild the bridge out of the loose boulders, with some success. In about an hour, a rough bridge had been reconstructed, and we all walked over it and waited for the trucks to follow.

Then, out of nowhere, appeared... a taxicab. It was for Frank and me, we were informed; get in, and go home, and goodbye. We guessed that the officer in charge had some kind of radio communication and had decided to avoid the likely embarrassment of two Americans sitting in his convoy as it rolled into the city, so he had ordered the cab for us. We accepted the favor with true gratitude. A cab home, even a battered, old one, seemed like a luxurious way to conclude our weekend holiday, so although Peace Corps volunteers did not ordinarily ride in cabs, we more than willingly shut up, got in, and said good bye.

We arrived back at our apartment at 8:30. There had been one more detour because one mile out of the city a river covered the road we had taken and we had to backtrack. We had been on the road from Ghazni for about fifteen hours and were hungry, exhausted, and a little bit dazed. Both of us vowed never to venture out of Kabul again without first carefully planning how we would go where we needed to go and making sure that those plans had some chance of fulfillment.

Which is what we did, with no better results, of course. The American belief that one can and should plan the future in order to assure a favorable outcome dies hard. Afghans had learned better, centuries before.

We later learned that our fellow volunteers had also chosen to travel that weekend, and that the rain that Saturday night had flooded roads everywhere. Bob and Roz Pearson had been stranded on a bandit-frequented road at 10:30 when the axle of their rented car broke. The nurses in our group had gone to Bamiyan and had to wade flooded rivers to get back.

I had to go back and forth from Kabul to Mazar-i-Sharif four times, as I will explain in a later chapter, and the first three of those trips were far more difficult than the trip to Ghazni. That explains why I twice chose to wait over two weeks to catch a plane instead of getting in, or on, one more earthbound vehicle.

Mazar-i-Sharif

OUR PEACE CORPS GROUP ARRIVED IN SEPTEMBER OF 1962, the smallest Peace Corps group before or since. As mentioned, the Afghan government was trying to maintain strict neutrality in the Cold War, its government walking a very careful path when it came to having foreign workers and volunteers in the country.

There were small German, French, and British communities, working primarily in health and education. There were embassies from various nations of both the Eastern and Western blocs; the Czech embassy was well known for occasionally having supplies of excellent Budoweiser beer for sale. But there were thousands of Russians and Americans, working in ministries and industries, in construction, in hospitals, in farming, in transportation, and in schools. The Soviets being understandably sensitive about their southern border, the Amu Darya (Oxus) River, Americans kept out of the northern provinces but had a large presence in Kandahar and Lashkar Gah, in the south.

In Kabul there were many representatives from both the East and West, but they rarely mixed socially. The image of the "Ugly American," a figure isolated from local culture and then prevalent in U.S. imaginations, was essentially false. It was the Russians who were isolated. True, Americans, while able to travel freely, were inclined to fall back on provisions from the U.S. commissary and thus avoid the local shops, while the Soviet commissary did not have the same kinds of goodies available, which forced the Russians to frequent the food bazaars. Yet the Russians essentially lived in a ghetto of their own making, and Russian wives went shopping *en masse*, escorted on one of their own buses. Because the Soviet Union contained many states (now independent ones) which shared cultures and traditions with Afghanistan, many Soviet citizens, although not able to travel freely even in their own country, were fairly familiar with the Afghan lifestyle. Yet they were looked down upon, not only because they stayed segregated but because, when they did venture into local shops, they bargained like paupers, offering too little and refusing to pay what Afghans considered a fair price, let alone the amounts Americans were willing to spend.

▼▼▼▼▼▼

In any case, the Afghan government was careful to balance the presence and influence of the eastern and western blocs, whose assistance was critical to them. The English-language Kabul Times always accompanied an article about the U.S. with one about the Soviet Union. If there was a visitor in the capital from Russia, that visit would receive a write-up, but there would also be an article of equal size about some development in the U.S. Ariana Airlines flew American planes with American-trained pilots; the other major airline using Kabul airport was Aeroflot. Unfortunately, the Soviet presence continued to grow in later decades until it was so overwhelming an influence on the Afghan economy and culture that socialism became a dominating political force, leading to a conservative reaction, a counter-reaction, and eventually invasion and civil war. The Cold War, as far as Afghanistan was concerned, actually created a precarious balance of influence that benefited the country as long as neither rival power could prevail.

Thus, when the Americans proposed sending a Peace Corps contingent to Afghanistan, there was a considerable delay and discussion before the Afghan government agreed to accept a total of thirteen volunteers, a small enough contingent so the Soviets would not feel threatened by an increased American presence. Our job, as that first small group, was to demonstrate that we were what we were supposed to be, volunteer workers, not spies. (We were told that a Russian broadcast, shortly before we arrived, had suggested that we were spies and could be so identified because we would be using cigarette lighters which were actually recording or communications devices, a clever suggestion which might easily have been believed had more than a couple of us been smokers).

So it was with a great degree of satisfaction that we were told, after our first evaluation, that we had succeeded entirely in winning over the Afghan government to accepting more volunteers. In fact, their first request that winter for thirty additional volunteers to arrive in June of 1963 had to be filled by the Peace Corps "stealing" nineteen teachers and seven printers from a group training for Ceylon. After only a few months of our presence, it was a surprising validation of our success. Moreover, by the time Afghan II and later Afghan III arrived, the government was comfortable about volunteers moving out of the capital into the provinces. Thus it was, just after the schools closed in Kabul in December of 1963, that I was joined by two new volunteers from Afghan II group in becoming the first Americans to work in Mazar-i-Sharif, a city of about 30,000 then, not far from the northern border.

Getting to and from Mazar was a whole separate story, which I will document elsewhere to illustrate again why it is that invading military forces invariably fail to control Afghanistan, since it is almost impossible to travel even short distances in the country. There was a regular bus service to Mazar, as well as private buses and flights on Ariana Afghan Airlines, but none of these functioned with any regularity. Nevertheless, after considerable delay, on December 21 I was ensconced in something called the Bakhdi Hotel on the city's main square, opposite the mosque. The government had torn down some old and decrepit housing about a year before in order to create a very handsome square and park surrounding the blue-tiled mosque. It was much finer than any of the mosques in Kabul, a site of pilgrimage for Shiite Moslems, since it is purported to be the burial place of the Prophet's son-in-law, Ali, whose death was responsible for the schism between the Shiite and Sunni branches of Islam. (It is not the only place where he is supposed to be buried, just as one can find two sites for the tomb of Jesus in Jerusalem and enough pieces of the true cross throughout Europe to build a small village.)

I had been preceded to Mazar by Charlotte and Ken Rand, a couple from Afghan II, who had selected the hotel and negotiated a room. It took me a while to talk the hotel owner down to what I considered a reasonable price, about 40 cents a day. My explanation that I would be guaranteeing him a rental for two months and so should pay less than the regular rent fell on deaf ears, since he insisted that the hotel might be full at some point, and at that point he would lose money on my room. Eventually he went along with my offer as long as I accepted a smaller than normal room, about 8 ft. by 10 ft., one previously used for wood storage. The claustrophobic proportions of the room were no particular problem, since there was no central heating in the hotel; a small wood stove with a vent through the window kept this smaller room passably warm.

The Rands and I had the use of a western-style bathroom, which we were allowed to keep padlocked while we made use of it. Not long after we arrived, however, the pipes froze, so we had to fill the basin and toilet from a huge tank of water which the hotel replenished every few days. The bathroom had, oddly enough, a bidet. It may have been used by some of the Afghans to wash before prayers, but it was not mistaken as a toilet. We knew the toilets were being used on occasion because we found shoe prints on the seat; Afghans, remember, normally squat instead of sit, and the kinds of squat-toilets found in other Asian countries were not used in connection with indoor plumbing in Afghanistan, so they used western toilets as best they could.

The hotel also had a large restaurant serving standard meals of *pilau* with a little lamb in it. When we grew tired of *pilau*, Charlotte Rand sometimes cooked in her room with a kerosene stove, and later, after the Rands had departed, I sometimes cooked a little for myself on a Primus stove, especially during *Ramazan*, when the restaurant was closed.

When I arrived the weather was mild and pleasant; Mazar is north of Kabul but at a lower altitude, so it has a milder climate, excellent for sheep raising. But on Christmas day the *shemali*, or north wind, arrived, followed a few days later by snow, followed by warmer weather and solid mud in the streets, and that alternating cold and warm, snow and mud, was the pattern for the months to come.

I worked at a "middle" school, grades 4 - 8, doing some teaching and some observation of Afghan teachers of English. My teaching load was light, but the two native teachers at the school had light loads too, amounting to about 32 hours per week between them. I was there, as in Kabul, not so much because there was enough work to justify my presence but simply to demonstrate that my presence was no threat to Afghan-Soviet friendship. I was laying the groundwork for other volunteers to come, especially in the smaller towns nearby where English teachers were hard to find. Still, because of the political realities, I was not supposed to travel very much, not at all towards the north and the border, so during much of my stay in Mazar, I was hibernating as often as working.

This was especially true when the Rands departed. We all traveled back to Kabul in January: Sergent Shriver, head of the Peace Corps and JFK's brother-in-law, was making a tour and our presence was requested, although not demanded. In spite of the inconvenience of travel, we made the effort to get back to Kabul and meet Shriver; he was a celebrity of sorts, and this was only a few months after Kennedy had been assassinated. We had, in a month, become bored enough with life in Mazar to look forward to the bright lights and thrills of being back in a city with a real restaurant and warm housing. The Rands were scheduled to begin their next assignment in February, but I had no long-term assignment, since I was scheduled to leave in May, so I returned to Mazar alone, where I spent a lonely period of doing very little (the schools closed by one o'clock during *Ramadan*) except waiting several weeks for transportation back to Kabul in March.

The Rands were from Texas, and we had little in common. We tolerated each other but did not become fast friends. He looked at me, I imagine, as an over-intellectual snob, a typical frat-boy Ivy Leaguer. I looked at him as a semi-yahoo Texan, full of bluster and bluff but not much education. I once got in a heated argument with him about his assertions that the appendix is on the-left hand side of the body and that Houston is closer to Teheran than Paris (there was no way we could settle the argument in Mazar, lacking anything like reference books or an atlas.) I was a bit taken aback when he said that he didn't like Shakespeare because he had once read Hamlet and found that it was too simple to be of interest. Still, I realized, he was hugely successful as a Peace Corps volunteer, for he had all the gregarious vitality, good spirits and boundless energy which I lacked and which represents one of the best features of Americans abroad. He had more Afghan friends than I did; not knowing where one's appendix is located is no drawback to making friends in a foreign country.

The saving grace was the friendliness of the teachers at my school. Most of them had never met anyone from the U.S. Many of them had never been more than a few miles from Mazar-i-Sharif. The two English teachers had learned their language in Afghanistan, from Indian teachers with texts prepared for Indian students, and it was those texts which they used. One of them had a fair mastery of English, but the other had only a rudimentary grasp, so his teaching consisted for the most part of reading out loud to his students from the text while they followed along, and then telling them what it said. All I could really do was suggest some ways to involve the students more in the process and try, without embarrassing him, to explain some of his obvious confusions.

For example, there is a basic discrepancy between Dari and English in the number of vowel sounds. Dari has about eight; English has thirteen, as I recall. Most Afghans pronounce the sounds in "bad" and "baud" the same as the sound in "body," and there are other necessary compromises of pronunciation unless one really drills in the unfamiliar sounds of English, something that does not happen unless a teacher is trained to do this. I observed one teacher trying to explain to his class the difference between the word "hill" and the word "hall," both of which appeared in the text. But his pronunciation of both words was a compromise, the closest he could come, since the vowels in those two words are not common in Dari. What he said to his students sounded, to me, like this: "This is a 'hell,' and this is a 'hell.' See? A 'hell' is like a mountain, and a 'hell' is outside this room. Repeat: 'I climbed up the hell. I walked down the hell to my classroom.' Very good."

The school buildings in Mazar were older, colder, and less well furnished that those in Kabul. Each room was heated by a small wood stove, of little comfort except to students sitting next to it. Cold had not been a problem in Kabul, since the schools closed in winter, but even in the milder climate of Mazar-I-Sharif, cold seeped into one's body as the day went on. The courtyards outside of classrooms, when the sun was out, were usually more comfortable than the small, dark rooms where I taught.

At the school's front entrance was what passed as the library. It was a tall, glass-fronted bookcase with a variety of materials inside, mostly English texts, novels, a few other resources such as dictionaries, an atlas or two, and other books in Dari or Arabic. The bookcase was locked and, as far as I could discover, would always remain locked. Its contents were too valuable to risk being taken out. Like the towels at Masdurat, the desks at Lycee Nadirya, and the rags at Zenda-ba-non, anything which was scarce was carefully guarded from possible theft or damage. The scarcer the resource, the less likely it would ever be used.

Other than teach, there was really nothing for me to do in Mazar. There was one movie theater that showed only Indian films, and old ones at that. Indian films are almost always musicals, and one which I saw a couple of times was a sort of combination of an Arabian nights swashbuckler and Three Stooges comedy, with songs and dances. That is, there was a great deal of chasing around on horseback, and sword fighting, and climbing up towers, a couple of fat men who acted foolishly and bumped into each other, and veiled women who sang. It played for weeks, and the Afghans loved it, although they could understand the dialogue no better than I. Like me, of course, they had nothing much to do, so any diversion at all seemed highly entertaining.

Another diversion for me was the presence of one American-educated Afghan, Hassan Alif, married to an American, Teresa, living in Mazar and working for the oil exploration company. He was more than gracious and hospitable, of course, as all Afghans are, and his wife was obviously lonely and isolated, although she never admitted this. She had met him when he attended college in Colorado, and, like many other American women, fallen in love with a handsome foreigner without fully realizing what life in his native country might be like. She told me of her first weeks in Kabul, having to sit quietly in the family home while visitors came and went, observing her, speaking with her in a language she only faintly understood, unable to go out or meet other Americans. Having moved to Mazar, she was even more isolated, having little in common with other Afghan wives in the community and having nothing much to do with her time.

I was invited to their house for dinner on several occasions, a much-anticipated break from my Primus stove or the one standard meal at the restaurant. On one occasion, I arrived to find that Hassan had another visitor, an old friend who lived miles away and had just happened to drop in. While Hassan and his visitor conversed in the living room, I chatted with Teresa in the kitchen, and an hour passed, and then another hour, and we all got very hungry. But she could not cook dinner because the visitor might either want to stay or to go home. He was invited to have dinner, but he couldn't make up his mind, and it would have been terribly impolite to insist that he do so. Or to go ahead and serve dinner. So we waited, and waited, and finally she decided it was long past time for dinner and started to cook. At that point the visitor decided he wanted to go home, and Hassan left to drive him there, a trip that took nearly an hour on the dark, snow-covered roads. It was a revelation of how deep the roots of hospitality ran in Afghan culture and also of what a burden it must have been for Hassan's wife. Even though Hassan understood and acknowledged how difficult her role was, he was a product of his culture and unable to help her escape from it.

My ten weeks in Mazar were not onerous, but there were times when, confined to my tiny room by cold, wind, and the absence of any reason to venture outside, I found days stretching on endlessly. During *Ramazan*, when the city was mostly shut down during the daylight hours, I read for hour after hour, often huddled in my bed when my small stove was inadequate to cut the chill. I cannot imagine what Hassan's wife, Teresa, found to do while he was at work. Her life must have been much like the lives of American pioneer wives isolated on small homesteads in winter. True, she did have a city around her, but the city had neither family nor friends sharing any common experience. Shops sold only identical common objets, such as pots and pans, water pipes, or foodstuffs. Afghan leisure time is spent with one's family, and she had none. Her life must have been unspeakably lonely, with nothing to look forward to except the eventual arrival of children.

In December of 1965, I received a sad letter from Hassan. After I arrived home the year before, I had sent him a package of American baking mixes and chocolate as a Christmas gift, but, I learned, they had not reached him until the following June. I also learned that he had been transferred to Kabul the previous July, shortly after I left Afghanistan, but in March of 1965 he had been required to join the Afghan army. Realizing what this would mean for his wife, he sent her back to Colorado, and, he wrote, "I've been living a bachelor's life ever since which is awfully hard." This must have been especially difficult for him, since his wife gave birth to their son in October. "Believe me, David, I feel so lonesome for my wife and son...." he wrote. He hoped to be able to travel after his army service and visit old friends in Colorado. I can only wonder if he was able to do that, if Teresa was willing to return to Afghanistan with him after a year back in America, and if they were ever reunited. He had sacrificed for his country, and she had sacrificed for him, and they deserved a happy ending to their story.

One Friday, we were able to drive in his jeep out to see Balkh, the ruin of the "mother of cities" that had once been a major stop on the silk route across Asia. I had looked forward to this visit; the ruins of ancient civilizations remind me of what life is really like and how short a time frame we individuals are allowed in the great scheme of things. But Balkh was more of a ruin than I had anticipated. Extensive mud walls, stretching out in all directions, with the remains of low watch towers at their corners; the front of a huge mosque, taller than any of the active mosques I had seen, but only a facade; a few ruins of two- or three-story building whose purpose could not be determined. Thousands, maybe hundreds of thousands of people had lived here. It had been a crossroads of civilization. And now, as with the silent statue of Shelley's "Ozymandias,"

... nothing beside remains.
Of that colossal wreck. Boundless and bare,
The low and level sands stretch far away.

On the Road Again

IT MIGHT SEEM THAT I HAVE ALREADY DWELT ENOUGH on the difficulties of travel in Afghanistan. Obstacles encountered nearly forty years ago might not be especially relevant today. After all, only one year after I left, I received a letter from another member of my group, Jan Mueller (who had married a volunteer from Afghan II and decided to remain another year) in which she mentioned that the road to the north was now paved. One could reach the border in only 8 hours, less than half the time it took only a year before for a 400-mile trip, soon to be further shortened by almost 100 miles when the Salang Tunnel was completed.

But that road is now heavily mined. Much of it was shelled during the decade when Russian convoys used it. There has been no money to maintain it for over almost two decades. And the Salang Tunnel, a major

Soviet engineering feat cutting through the mountains, was mined during the civil wars and became essentially unusable.

Nothing is any more important to understanding Afghanistan than the fact that the core of the country is a mass of mountain peaks cut by steep, rocky gorges. Around that central mass are foothills where sheep can graze and valleys where crops can be adequately watered, but only a small percent of the land is arable. Still further from the mountains, especially in the south, there are barren deserts. Transportation by anything other than camel, donkey, or walking is unreliable at best and horrendously slow in any case. Vehicles break down from cold, from horrendously rough roads, from being manned by inept and untrained drivers, from old age, from poor fuel, and from improvised repairs or lack of any repair at all.

The impassable terrain is a hindrance to armies, of course, as every invader has discovered. It is equally a hindrance to the development of the country's trade, economy, and political cohesion. Peoples who cannot easily travel do not know neighbors more than a few miles away; physically isolated tribes are not likely to form a nation in any modern sense of the word.

Looking over my old letters, I note that virtually every time I ventured out of Kabul, except for short excursions on holidays with Americans (preferably Americans with jeeps) there was no certainty that I would arrive on the day or even during the week for which I had planned. My worst experiences occurred in December of 1963 when I went to Mazar-i-Sharif and then in January when I decided to return to Kabul so that I could meet with other volunteers greeting Sargent Shriver on his world tour. Two round trips to Mazar, and not one of them went as planned.

My original move to Mazar was first scheduled for a December Monday, but I had a test to give that day, one last exam before the Kabul schools closed. So I did not take the plane that the Rands, my fellow volunteers caught. The next flight was on Wednesday, but it was canceled because of cloudy weather in the mountains; the DC-3's in use could fly through the mountains but not over them. The Friday flight was canceled Thursday afternoon because of rain. The unpaved airport in Mazar, I learned, needed a day or two to dry out. Friday and Saturday were clear and dry, though, so I went to the airport and left on the scheduled Monday flight, which got to Mazar in about an hour and then turned around and flew back. The Mazar airfield was still wet and muddy, but nobody had thought of letting Kabul know that. Another flight was scheduled for Wednesday, but it was also canceled just as I was leaving for the airport. It was the following Friday when all the elements conspired so that I could actually take a plane as planned, a twelve day delay for a one-hour flight.

Not a single plane landed in Mazar for several weeks after that, but only a month later the Rands and I were advised that Shriver would be in Kabul, and if we could somehow get there it might provide a pleasant respite from our fairly bleak existence in the north. We knew by then that waiting for a plane would be futile, so we determined to travel by land. Four hundred miles, since we had not attempted it before, did not seem especially daunting. We had hoped that a truck from the Oil Exploration Company might be making the trip, but such trips were infrequent and unscheduled, so we threw caution to the winds and boarded one of the scheduled Russian buses operated by the government-sanctioned bus company which, we hoped, would prove more reliable than the private bus services run on no schedule at all.

We left Mazar at 8:30 in the morning and drove, with many interruptions, until 12:40 that night, with a one-hour stop for dinner in a tiny village and a few other short stops for prayers. Since it was *Ramazan*, the driver neither ate nor drank until it was dark, nor would we have except that the Afghans urged us not to feel any compunction about having a little bread in one of the towns we passed through. The driver, however, was showing clear signs of fatigue, and his ability to maneuver around the rocks, water, mud, gouges in the roadbed, snow and ice (without benefit of chains or special tires) was severely compromised. Blind curves often hid oncoming vehicles or stationary camels and donkeys, requiring the driver to brake suddenly, sending the bus into skids that caused Charlotte Rand to become increasingly terrified. Perhaps our fellow passengers were terrified, too, but if that was the case, they prayed silently. She managed with difficulty not to scream.

We did convince the driver to eat a little bread and to smoke in order to keep awake, but by the time we stopped at 12:40, he was clearly exhausted. Still, he told us he felt too sick to sleep, so only the passengers got some rest, until 3:45 A.M. when we took off again. We arrived in Kabul at 5:30 the next evening. Even in the summer, we learned, this is a trip most people avoid, but in the winter it was two days of unremitting, cold discomfort. I determined to return to Mazar by plane, no matter how long I had to wait. The Rands, who would be leaving for another assignment shortly thereafter, decided not to return at all.

A week later, no flight to Mazar had departed or been scheduled, and I was not accomplishing anything sitting around Kabul, so it was decided that, instead, I would fly to another northern city, Kunduz, and try to find a taxi or bus from there to Mazar so that the trip through the mountains, at least, could be avoided. It was supposed to be only an eight-hour drive between those two cities. And I did get to Kunduz, where the airport was paved. Kunduz was a fairly modern industrial city, by Afghan standards, with textile mills constructed with Russian help.

But the road from Kunduz to Mazar was impassable, I learned, because of snow. The winter of 1963 was one of the harshest in local memory. The only way to get to Mazar was to back-track to Pul-i-Khumri, a village to the north of the Hindu Kush where the roads to Mazar and Kunduz met, and so I found a truck to take me back to Pul-i-Khumri, which I had passed through a week before. That part of the trip was relatively easy, taking only about five hours, and I discovered that there was a very nice place to stay there, called the Nasanji Club, where it turned out that another volunteer was staying while he waited for his promised housing to develop. Thus I was able to sleep comfortably and be refreshed for the balance of the trip the next morning over much of the same mountainous terrain I had previously passed in the opposite direction, although only about half of the distance.

I could not discover any scheduled bus, however, and in any event I had not made a reservation. So at 7 A.M. I went to the area where buses were staging and eventually identified one expecting to go to Mazar. It left two hours later, when enough other passengers had collected for the driver to feel it worth while to depart. That meant that the bus was dangerously overloaded, and the roads were still covered with ice. This time the inevitable happened: at 4:15, many miles from Mazar, the bus skidded and overturned in the snow. Fortunately, the snow banks were high and soft, and so the bus only rolled onto its side, with no injuries to the passengers but no way for the bus to proceed. It promised to be a long, cold night in the middle of nowhere.

Then, in less than a quarter-hour, a small miracle occurred. One of the regularly scheduled buses appeared, and one other older passenger and I were encouraged to clamber aboard and make use of the two vacant places which could somehow be found. We did not protest too much. I understood that this was a typical example of Afghan hospitality, that I was a guest in the country, and therefore a guest of everyone, and anything less than insisting on my taking advantage of the bus would be an embarrassment. At any rate, I convinced myself that this was the case and boarded the bus, arriving back at my hotel in Mazar at 6 P.M. My luggage arrived the next day, safe and untouched, along with the other passengers whose night in the snowfields they seemed to accept as just one more unpredictable twist of fate. Afghans, by the way, always travel with bedrolls, and with good reason.

I determined I would wait for a plane back to Kabul when I finished my Mazar assignment, no matter how long it took. One plane had arrived during my stay, and spring was almost upon us, so I was sure the airport would become dry enough to go back into service. I was nearing the end of my service in Afghanistan, and it didn't matter all that much what day I got back to Kabul to take up some temporary teaching duties. So I waited. And waited. I read books. I looked out the window. I read some more. I wrote in my diary, noting that it hadn't rained, so the airport would certainly be clear, then learning it was clear, but than no flights were scheduled, then noting that it snowed, then watching the snow melt and hoping the mud would dry out, then watching another light rain fall, day after day. I waited almost two weeks and finally gave in.

My friend Hassan, who worked for the Oil Exploration Company, told me that this time, for sure, there would be a company bus leaving for Kabul the next day, and it should be nearly empty. He could reserve space for me and for all the Rands' belongings, which I had to transport to Kabul along with my own. The bus would be ready at 7 A.M. so I carefully packed everything up and was ready, bright and early the next morning. Some people never learn.

At 8:20 I got hold of my friend by telephone, after the operator insisted he didn't have one, to ask where the bus was, which he said he had sent a half-hour before. The bus has gone to some other hotel, it turned out, so the driver sent a jeep for me. The bus was not at all empty; it was crammed full, and so the driver had to reload it entirely to get my stuff and the Rands' stuff on.

At 10:20 the bus pulled out. At 10:25 it stopped for gas. Again I noted that planning ahead by filling the tank before loading the bus was not a priority in this culture.

Little children stood in the aisles, or sat on laps. Luggage and people were tossed around when the bus went over rough patches, which was most of the time. It was a small nightmare I had lived through before, except this time the progress was even slower. I kept careful notes that day which show that we stopped at 11:40 to adjust luggage, which was falling all over the passengers (it had been jammed into one front corner of the bus.) At 12:20 the driver stopped again to examine the engine, since the bus kept stalling when he tried to use high gear climbing a hill. At 12:30 we stopped for lunch in Tashkurgan. We stopped at Haibak at 3:30 and again stopped to pick up passengers at 4:15, in spite of the bus already being over-full. They sat on the front steps. At 4:20 we again stopped for gas. At 6:00 we stopped for prayers. At 7:05 we had to stop for half an hour because there was a truck with a broken axle in the middle of the road, necessitating that all of us help dig out a passage on the roadside to get around it. At 8:35 we pulled into Pul-i-Khumri, where the Nasanji Club beckoned, and I decided it would be prudent for me to get an actual night's sleep and hope I could find transportation back to Kunduz, going back to Kabul by air from there, the reverse of my trip north a month before. Our bus driver bus told me that he expected to get into Kabul the morning after the next one. I believed him and bailed out, telling him where to deliver my luggage.

There was one last land leg for me to travel, and that was by "taxi" to Kunduz. The only vehicle I could find the next morning was a jeep, which was fine, but like other vehicles for hire, it was not going to leave until it could stuff aboard the last possible body. That meant ten passengers, and it might take all day, or longer, to find ten passengers for Kunduz. I could have rented the whole vehicle, at ten times my own fare, but that was too American-rich style for a Peace Corps volunteer. Still, I had to get to Kunduz before the flight to Kabul left. After a while I convinced the driver that letting me pay five times the fare was probably a good deal for him, and he apparently thought that this represented the best kind of traditional haggling, so we took off, and even though he stopped for a couple of other passengers on the way (thus getting the best of the bargain) we arrived in time for me to make the flight, assisted in finding space because I knew one of the pilots. Several of the Peace Corps girls, after the country took a more liberal political stance the previous winter, dated Ariana pilots, and I had no qualms about taking advantage of that friendship. Personal relationships often grease the wheels in almost any country, especially in a country where there is little incentive for anyone to do anything except to extend favors to family and friends.

There is one last note from my diary of this trip, even though it has nothing to do with the subject of this chapter, which is the near-impossibility of anything approaching scheduled or comfortable travel in Afghanistan (a factor which is still in evidence when one reads of modern refugees struggling to get out of the country, often traveling for days on foot). It is a quote from the manager of the Nasanji club, a man trained in Germany. By day, he was a foreman in the local factory, so he actually held down two full-time jobs and was making about the same amount of money as I was as a Peace Corps volunteer, good wages for an Afghan. But, I pointed out to him, he was working night and day in order to do that.

"Here in Afghanistan, there is nothing to drink, no music, no women, no place to go," he responded. "Better to work."

Perhaps he had spent too much time in Germany.

Politics as Unusual

I N September of 2001, Americans suddenly became aware of this obscure country in central Asia when a fanatic named Osama Bin Laden, who was not an Afghan, and his gang of terrorists, most of whom were not Afghans, became the focus of American hatred because of the destruction of the World Trade Center.

In subsequent weeks we suddenly were slightly baffled trying to distinguish between Afghans and Arabs, Arabs and Muslims, the Taliban and the Afghan people they were terrorizing, Pathans and Pushtuns, Uzbekistan and Uzbeks, and all the other divisions of race, religion, and nationality which make up the patchwork quilt of nations and peoples once again involved in what was called, in the nineteenth century, "The Great Game."

This is not the place to try to recount the complicated and confusing history of central Asia, or even the equally complex and sometimes incomprehensible history of Afghanistan, but a small review of some of that history is necessary to have any understanding of current events in that part of the world. There are some very old, very important themes that we see recurring with which, if we are not careful and knowledgeable, we will find ourselves entangled.

From the late eighteenth century until World War II, European powers were engaged in a period of expansion through empire building, and two of those powers, Russia and Great Britain, became rivals in Asia. Russia slowly established hegemony over lesser nations to its east and south, while Britain, having colonized India, found itself drawn into the politics of the peoples surrounding its new empire, especially to the north. That rivalry helped to create many nations we recognize today but which had not existed as such previously. The borders of Turkey, Iraq, Iran, India, Pakistan, Bangladesh, and Myanmar were originally drawn primarily by European colonizers to serve as defensible military positions. Much later, after the collapse of the Soviet Union, republics such as Uzbekistan and Tadjikistan came into being. But before they had been absorbed into the Soviet Union in the 1920's they had not had stable governments, stable borders, or a sense of nationhood. It was the presence of the two great powers which served to bring together disparate groups of tribes to resist, to rebel, and to repel those powers. To a great extent, these nations came into being to oppose European colonialism.

The place we call Afghanistan was briefly subdued by Alexander the Great (the city of Kandahar derives its name from his; it was one of the many Alexandrias he founded). Centuries later much of the region became a center of Buddhist civilization and worship. After 622 CE, Islam exploded out of the Arabian peninsula, and within two hundred years it had spread its rule to much of central Asia and northern India. Ghengis Khan devastated these lands on his way west, and the Mongols continued to control most of this part of the world for centuries. Later the Mogul dynasty was founded in Kabul by Babur and conquered much of India; the Taj Mahal is a monument to the high artistic level that culture achieved . But there never was really a country called Afghanistan. Some of the Pushtun tribes, under various shahs, controlled parts of what is today southern Afghanistan and northern Pakistan, but the other tribes in "Afghanistan" did not see their region as a nation.

It was only when Russia and Great Britain, after having tried and failed to extend their influence in these lands through covert alliances or overt military intervention, recognized that the cost of controlling the area was too high to pay and decided to create Afghanistan as a buffer state between them. The northern border was drawn at the Oxus (or Amu Darya) River because it formed a natural barrier, even though nomadic tribes lived on both sides of the river and regularly crossed it. Those tribes, the Kazaks, Turkomen, Uzbeks, Kirghiz, and Tadjiks, did not distinguish their brethren across the river from themselves, and today there are still strong ties between tribes on both sides of this border. On the west, a line was drawn in the sand between Persia, now Iran, and Afghanistan; what makes it a border is primarily the difficulty of travel in the dry, wasted lands, and nothing else. To the east, a small finger of land was extended through the Pamir Knot, the mountains which connect the Hindu Kush to the Himalayas, for no other purpose than to link Afghanistan and China, so that Russia and India would not share a border of even a few miles. And, to the south, where the British drew the Durand Line, the border ran across mountain peaks so that the British could defend the Northwest Provinces from Pushtun raiders.

The Durand line divided tribes and even families without any regard to their true affiliations and feeling of nationhood. On the Afghan side, they are called Pushtuns, and on the Pakistani side they are called Pakhtuns (and in colonial British documents they were referred to as Pathans, which is generally considered an insulting term by the peoples themselves). When the British left India, and the peoples were given the choice of becoming part of India or Pakistan, the Pushtuns boycotted the election, demanding the choice of being part of Afghanistan or of forming their own nation, Pushtunistan, making up about half of present-day Pakistan. Even in 1962, when I served in Afghanistan, Afghan schools had maps that showed the existence of "occupied Pushtunistan," for which the main square in Kabul was named. There was a Pushtunistan flag, and an anthem played nightly on Radio Kabul, and the border with Pakistan was officially closed because of ongoing disputes about the right of Pakistani Pushtuns to claim independence.

Pushtunistan never gained the recognition of other nations and was considered by most of them a mythical country. Yet it existed in the minds of many who lived in Afghanistan and Pakistan, and even today most Pushtun and Pakhtun tribesmen identify themselves more by their tribal alliances than as part of any nation. To them, Afghanistan, the nation to the north of "Pushtunistan," was an artificial one, a collection of disparate peoples, ruled by a royal Pushtun oligarchy, with borders imposed by others. Pakistan was seen by them as new nation to the south that had usurped power over the tribes of the former Northwest Territories, adjacent to British-dominated India. To a large extent, these beliefs continue today, much as the various ethnic groupings which made up

"Yugoslavia" never perceived that nation as more than a collection of separate cultures, bound together by the wrongheaded mapmaking of other powers.

There have been many shahs, emirs, and kings in the lands of Afghanistan. Their rule has never been absolute, extending over all the territory of that land to any significant degree, and that rule was often dependent on the good will of the British Empire, which included financial subsidies to keep the peace on its northwest frontier. Afghanistan only officially became independent of Britain in 1919.

Most important to understand, there have been no rulers of Afghanistan since the death of Abdur Rahman 1901 who were not assassinated or overthrown. The last hundred years has seen a steady succession of attempts at modernization and reactions against it. Zahir Shah, the 87-year old former monarch who now resides north of Rome, became king, in name only, when his father, Nadir Shah, was assassinated at a high school ceremony in 1933. Nadir Shah had been a military leader, although related to one of the many lines of Afghan rulers. He overthrew a bandit ruler, called Bacha-e-Saqao ("son of the water carrier") who had, with the help of ultra-conservative mullahs, overthrown a progressive king, Amanullah, who had tried to model his rule of the country on Ataturk. Amanullah's father, Habibullah, was also assassinated, whether because he was modernizing the country or because of tribal rivalries is not certain.

When we arrived in Kabul in 1962, Zahir Shah was king, but it was common knowledge that it was his cousin, Muhammad Daud, the Prime Minister who held real power in the government. Zahir Shah had been only nineteen when he became king twenty-nine years before, and his uncles had ruled in his name while he went to France to gain an education. His reign had never been a rule; the monarchy was actually an oligarchy.

Under Zahir Shah (actually under Daud), the ruling family was trying to modernize, slowly and carefully, but this was still a difficult process, generally opposed by rural clerics who owned much of the land and saw any central power as a threat to their way of life.

In the spring of 1963, we heard rumors that there had been surprising developments within the government and, it eventually became evident, this had indeed been the case. Somehow, Zahir Shah had wrested control from his uncle and was eventually able to convene a Loy Jirga, or tribal council, which established a constitutional monarchy, providing for elections to a representative parliament. The border was reopened with Pakistan; police were no longer in evidence watching our houses; Afghans began to meet with us and interact more freely. It was a subtle, quiet revolution, but the word was out: Afghanistan was again moving in the direction of a free and open society.

Sadly, that change led to a slow move towards socialism, or, rather, the kind of pretended socialism which was then sponsored by the Soviets. In 1973, Daud managed to return to power and oust the king, who fled the country. Daud had once favored a closer association with his powerful neighbors to the north, whereas Zahir Shah, European educated, leaned towards the western democracies. But as the country drifted further and further towards the left, Daud began to fear the total domination of his country by the Soviet Union, and in 1978, his arrest of some communist leaders led to a coup, and to his death. Within a year, the communist party in power was threatened by an anti-communist revolution and the Russian army moved in, as it had on more than occasion in Eastern Europe, to prevent the collapse of a communist state. In due course the Russians were expelled; after a decade of bloodshed they no longer wanted to waste money and lives in this barren land. Americans, having supported the mujahedeen in expelling the Russians, washed their hands of the whole matter and left the tribes, now armed with modern technology, to kill one another, which they proceeded to do.

Eventually it was a group known as the Taliban which emerged and managed to gain control of 90% of the country. Unfortunately, this group was largely composed of uneducated primitive rural mullahs, not at all representative of the educated middle-class Afghans who formed ministries under earlier governments. Most of those had fled the country during one or the other internecine wars of the previous two decades. As had occurred when Amanullah was expelled, bandits were in power, supported by the most reactionary mullahs in the countryside. Like all other rulers of the country, they depended largely on financial support from outside their borders. But unlike the emirs of previous centuries, whose support came from the British or Russians, or later from the United States and European powers, the new rulers were financed by the new oil-wealthy Arab nations and their dependents. Saudi Arabia, it seems, had provided most of the money to the Taliban, and Pakistan had provided most of the muscle. It is that muscle which has destroyed the country; the bandits of earlier times had no tanks or Stinger missiles.

And so it is unusual politics, as usual, in Afghanistan. The pendulum swung throughout the last century between modernization and a return to medieval primitivism. The country, even in 2001, has more in common with the Middle Ages than with the new century: about 90% of the population is engaged in agriculture, about 90% is illiterate; transportation is by donkey and camel more than by auto or truck; religious education is the only kind available to the mass of the population and is used by religious leaders to promote a primitive submission to the will of God. Questioning is, in itself, an irreligious act, for all answers are either already known or cannot be known, since only God can determine what will happen.

Like European kingdoms, princedoms, dukedoms, marches, and baronies of 1400, there is a common religion, but there is no common culture extending beyond the distance a man can travel in a day. The mass of people know only what they are told. Most of these people want only to survive the pointless battles between powerful chiefs who wage brutal war destroying their farmlands for unknowable reasons.

There has never been real cohesion within the Afghan borders. There are as many Pushtuns in Pakistan as in Afghanistan, possibly more, given recent immigration. Some have relatives who are associated with the Taliban, some have resided in Pakistan for generations and feel no connection with their primitive cousins across the mountains, and some have relatives who have resided for several generations in America or Europe. Similarly, there are residents in Uzbekistan who feel close ties to Afghan Uzbeks, and some who feel none, and some who have long since been accustomed to Russian traditions. The same could be said for tribes of Tadjiks, Turkomen, and Kazakhs.

In the central regions of Afghanistan live the Hazaras, a Mongolian group who observe the Shiite branch of Islam, rather than the majority Sunni branch. Long discriminated against by many of their countrymen, they have nothing in common with the predominant Pushtuns tribes who for so long ruled the country. In the northeast of the nation, the region called Nuristan, live a people who were pagan until they were forcefully converted at the end of the nineteenth century, many of them blond and blue-eyed, possibly descendants of Alexander's Greek soldiers. And on all the fringes of the country live the *koochis*, the nomads and gypsies of the country, who have for centuries roamed across the borders with their flocks as the seasons dictated.

Politics as usual means that there is no real government of Afghanistan. There never has been a powerful central government. Even when I was there during a period of steady modernization, there was no national transportation system, a rudimentary economic policy, a rudimentary education system, some taxation of some lands, and an inadequate system of communication. The army was a joke. Outside the capital, government influence was tenuous at best. There was a thin veneer of safety for most people and a government police force that could maintain some order, some of the time. But many government workers worked without steady pay for long periods. American and other foreign aid was essential to maintaining health and trade.

Yet food supplies were adequate. Drought or crop failure were not common occurrences. A high rate of infant mortality kept the population small, in comparison with the teeming millions of Pakistan and India to the south. There was only a very tiny upper class, and that class did not live in anything like luxury, so that what little the land produced was distributed more equitably than in modernized neighboring countries. Starvation and poverty were relatively uncommon in Afghanistan before civil wars destroyed the economy. Beggars were rare in Kabul when I lived there; our Peace Corps volunteers who visited India were appalled by omnipresent begging there.

Years of war have stripped away that veneer, and the country is now back, approximately, where it was in 1932. Probably it is much worse off, since so much of the irrigation system has been ruined and so many fields have been taken out of active cultivation because of the presence of mines. Afghanistan went from a developing country to a devastated one, from one slowly adopting modern ways to a medieval land with technology limited to weapons of war. Perhaps other technology can be reintroduced again swiftly, if money is made available. But it will take years to re-establish the infrastructure necessary to make that technology useful. Even more than when I lived there, mechanics need to trained, and teachers, and nurses, and printers, and clerks, and engineers, and all the other people without whose basic skills technology is useless.

We are faced with trying to find a way to introduce a modern, technological democracy to a land that, like medieval Europe, has no basis for creating a civilization beyond that of a local village. But there is an important difference. Unlike Europe in the thirteenth century, Afghanistan has already experienced its Renaissance. And, under a fanatical religious tyranny, been forced to turn its back on it.

Working with Washington

Y TOUR OF DUTY, SOME OTHER
ere invited to write an article
ine, The Volunteer, about our
e an issue devoted mostly to
urse that issue appeared. But
e no copy of it. I do, however,
tter to our regional director,
in Washington whose name
vorking for the government.
This letter read, in part:

"Thanks to you all for your help on the section. It seems to me a shame that Fleishhacker's piece was not permitted to run. My superiors (and yours) felt that the implied criticisms were dangerous... The Volunteer can never be a great publication because the pieces that would make it great will never get printed."

I have only a dim recollection of writing that article, but I have a fair idea of what the "criticisms" referred to must have been, and they were not criticisms of the Afghan government, or the Afghan people, or the volunteers. They were criticisms of the Washington bureaucracy which, even in a mold-breaking organization like the Peace Corps, represented America at its most mediocre.

My diary recorded many examples of such mediocrity. It began with our training, which was mostly excellent, bringing together scholars of Afghan history and culture, language experts, and Afghans in the U.S. to prepare us, and prepare us well, for our adventures in an unfamiliar culture. For ten hours a day, six days a week, we spent eight weeks intensively studying these, with extra language training added to fill some of the time caused by delays in our arrival, and additional language study after we arrived in Kabul. All this was to the good. But we also had to endure something called American Studies and World Studies, taking up two hours a day some weeks. We were all college educated. Most of us had traveled outside the U.S. What we were exposed to was essentially the content of a high-school civics class, with a smattering of propaganda thrown in, including a brochure I still own called "Notes on the Language of Communism," specially written for the Peace Corps. It felt to us as if the Peace Corps was not really sure that self-selected volunteers could be trusted out of the country without a refresher course on our government and the world at large. These classes, in contrast to those given by experts about Afghanistan, were pitched at the lowest possible level, containing nothing to stimulate thought or provide serious discussion by the college graduates forced to endure them. If this is typical of the kind of training our foreign service workers receive, we thought, how can they hope to interact with representatives of other nations, given a background with such shallow perspective?

In one trivial regard, some of us even rebelled. We were expected to report for PE classes before breakfast every morning and do laps around the Georgetown field. Some of us enjoyed sports and didn't mind this. I was three years out of college, and I had long since realized that I was no athlete. Planning to live in a city and teach, I saw no reason to change my routine of physical non-fitness significantly, and since our PE classes only began at the point when a 340-member group training for service in Ethiopia joined us, I realized on the first day that my absence would not be noted. So I skipped the second day and every day after that, and soon most of my fellow volunteers were sleeping in also. I never had a sick day during my two years abroad, during which my life made no greater demands on my physical fitness than my life in San Francisco had.

After training, we were prepared for the possibility that there would be delays in our departure, as there were, but there was no reason to blame Washington for these, which resulted from trying to establish an entirely new American presence in a sensitive region. Our training was extended, and we were sent to Lancaster, Pennsylvania, to attend a conference of Afghan students, probably the best use of time that could be arranged on short notice. Our travel arrangements allowed us to spend a couple of days in New York and part of a day in Rome, and it was certainly not Washington's fault that we also had to spend three days in Teheran.

But some of the simplest details that we expected would be handled with normal competence were snafued. Many of our trunks were not picked up until after we had left, which meant that we had to live with our 44-lb. allotment of luggage for months. On the other hand, sets of encyclopedias (which we were happy to have, but did not desperately need) arrived immediately. We were stuck in the Kabul Hotel for nearly two months while our director argued with Washington about housing arrangements. As mentioned before, Washington wanted us dispersed all over the city in separate houses, while Bob Steiner argued, ultimately successfully, that Afghans lived in extended, large family groups in houses not designed for single dwellers, that our work places were mostly in one area, and that the five single women in our group could not safely or comfortably live alone. We were dismayed to discover so soon upon arrival that the Washington staff assumed they should make decisions which they had no competence to make.

Even in little things, Washington made determinations which anyone living in Kabul could see were ill-advised. They shipped a jeep for our director to use; many jeeps were for sale locally at reasonable prices. They sent us vitamin pills, but these were prenatal capsules, adequate, but hardly designed for our needs. They wired us long news reports which contained nothing we could not derive from local sources, but promised copies of Time, Life, and the New York Times, which we really craved, failed to arrive because we had no street addresses.

It was not very long before the first of many Washington evaluators arrived. Governments love to collect facts and statistics to demonstrate that they are doing a good job. We were not required to fill out endless forms or file reports; in that regard, the Peace Corps maintained its slightly rebellious, no-nonsense style. Still, it was a controversial new program, and that meant that somebody had to evaluate something, somehow. I am sure my article was censored because I criticized the way this was done. Evaluators arrived regularly from Washington, none of whom had been exposed to the kind of training we had undergone, none of whom was familiar with the country, its culture, or its language. Hence, all they could do was to talk to us, or our supervisor, or government officials, and then interpret what they heard, or misheard through their own preconceptions. In the many interviews I had with people from our government, it was clear that they did not really know what questions to ask. They would have needed at least a month to begin to get a feel for the local scene in order to understand how we were living or what we were doing, but, in typical American fashion, they breezed into town for a few days, ran around and talked to as many people as they could, and then breezed out again. They made suggestions based on what they had observed in other countries, unaware of how inappropriate and unreasonable much of what they offered was for our particular circumstances.

Not that they were critical or sent back negative reports. Our group actually received very positive evaluations, and the fruits of our labors became immediately apparent when the Afghan government, after having been reticent six months before to request even thirteen volunteers, was suddenly requesting thirty more to arrive as soon as possible. Less than two years after we had arrived, the Peace Corps in Afghanistan numbered 165 volunteers. We must have been doing well, and the evaluators must have realized that. Still, the kinds of questions asked during interviews with Washington staff and the implication that they felt capable of judging us, lacking any background preparing them to do this, rankled.

The summer after we arrived our director went on vacation. This did not create any special needs, since by then we were all fully involved in our regular work and were not supervised at all by the local Peace Corps office. Still, Washington sent someone out to run things, and he managed to create far more antagonism than he realized by arguing with some of the volunteers, from the very first night, about matters he could not understand without at least a smattering of experience. In the long run, he did "get it" and eventually became part of the staff in Kabul. The same could not be said for another member of the Washington staff who had visited for a few days a month earlier. We were appalled at his lack of depth. He asked some of us why we ate potatoes instead of rice. He asked how many of the books (not which books) sent by the Peace Corps we had read. I was personally deeply offended by his writing our director, after he left, that he heard I had been using my own money for luxuries, an allegation that he had not had the courtesy, or the guts, to discuss with me. We have all become familiar with the malicious gossip often pervading government, but this was my first personal encounter with it, and I was appalled.

At the end of my tour of duty, there was a possibility that I could continue in Kabul in a staff position. I had grown to enjoy my life there, and I gave it serious consideration for a while. But what I had come to understand about too many expatriate workers for the U.S. Government discouraged me from joining their ranks. I had been to too many cocktail parties where behavior was rude and comments about the local population, from people who did not know them well, were ill-considered. I was surprised to see how many traditional Christians there were in the community, Christians who had not seemed to learn much about the values of their hosts. I was so taken aback by one of our hosts at a dinner in Kabul that I wrote down his comments. He maintained that Afghans lacked the Christian virtue of brotherly love (apparently blind to the fundamental Afghan virtue of hospitality to strangers). And then he went on with the following non-sequiter: "Think of what *Ramazan* would do to business and trade in the U.S."

I returned to the United States and for the next thirty-five years have lived my life immersed in the pleasures of enjoying our consumerist life-style. I like my warm home, my television sets, my CD players and computers, my cars, my freedom, my comfort. I also know what it is like to live without them. And lack of that knowledge, I often think, is what makes too many Americans, especially those in the government, narrow of view in the most important sense.

Americans think that the world is pretty much like our own country, only poorer. That's not it at all.

People who work within the Washington beltway think the United States, is pretty much like Washington. That's not it, either.

Most of the people of the U.S. could live happy, productive, and comfortable lives without 90% of the regulations which come out of Washington and the endless record keeping and paper-shuffling which accompanies them. Most of the people of the world would go on with their lives in about the same way whether or not the United States existed. It is not so much our arrogance as a nation that others dislike, although there is plenty of that. It is our ignorance. Even though we supply millions of dollars of aid to other countries, we often do so ignorantly, the decisions on the form and substance of such aid being made by people with no knowledge of the countries for which that aid is intended. We create the same antagonism in foreign nations as we often can find at home when Washington imposes regulations on states and cities that fit national political agendas but are ill-suited to the needs of the people most directly affected.

We could do so much better, and so easily. In spite of never-ending criticisms of the American education system, it is the finest in the world. The clearest evidence is two-fold: the number of Nobel Prize winners from the United States is far out of proportion to our population, and students from every country seek to enter our universities.

Our educational system attracts and welcomes students from abroad. Moreover, people living abroad are familiar with our culture, albeit through a distorted lens, from the profusion of American films, TV, and music which is distributed in every land. Conversely, however, only a small proportion of our best students study abroad. Americans have little exposure to or interest in the films, TV, or music of other lands, especially non-European nations. A large proportion of Americans who live abroad are in the military, and they often live on bases which are American ghettos, insulated from the local culture.

Other nations have large expatriate colonies in America who can provide information to their relatives at home. The city of Fremont, across the bay from San Francisco, claims an Afghan population of about 40,000, for example. There must be hundreds of thousands of Afghans living in the United States, not to mention millions who live in other countries. How many Americans have ever lived in Afghanistan for more than a few months? How many have lived for an extended time in any country? A relative handful, at most. We are a nation of immigrants; that is our strength. Yet it also means that, except for those of us who emigrated here recently, we profoundly lack a knowledge and understanding of other countries. Our elected and appointed officials, on the whole, have lived their entire lives in an American bubble, with American blinders, and when they try to think about other countries, they lack the kind of understanding which can only be acquired by experience, not in a classroom. Whatever other qualities of mind and character our current President may have brought to the office, he had never traveled abroad. He represents all too well, sad to say, an American lack of interest in the rest of the world.

In times of peace our country, self-sufficient in most ways, has often wished for a simpler world, one where we need not know much about or do much about what is happening elsewhere. We entered World War II reluctantly, but the lessons of that war led to our involvement in reconstructing Europe through the Marshall Plan, not really a selfless action, but a brilliant and effective tactic to create a world where our kind of civilization could flourish. After Vietnam, as after World War I, the national mood was to retreat and retrench, to dismantle our intelligence operations and avoid entanglements abroad. After the end of the Cold War, we hoped that most international matters had been settled for all time. Then, one September morning, we learned yet again that we are a part of the world, neither masters of it nor isolated in a corner of it. We must constantly seek to understand and be involved, intelligently, with every corner of the globe. Ignorance is not a choice, and power without wisdom is no power at all.

We are on the top of the mountain, looking down, and we can't see all the details making up the landscape. It is in the details that truth resides. Working in the Peace Corps, down at the bottom of the mountain, I understood what it felt like when the visitors from Washington looked down at us and could not see what they stayed too distant from to observe. It is a lesson we, as a nation, need to learn as well.

▼▼▼▼▼▼

Dope

I T IS DIFFICULT TODAY TO REALIZE HOW NAIVE I WAS, how naive all of us were, about drugs back then. That was 1962, remember. We were white, middle-class or upper-class young adults. None of us had ever known anyone who used any kind of drugs other than tobacco or alcohol. We knew that some people were addicted to heroin; we believed that a few deranged people sniffed cocaine. We knew there was something called marijuana, which people smoked, but we did not distinguish it from other drugs, or know why anyone would choose to be drugged in any way.

Nobody spoke to us about drugs during training. I doubt than any of the people who trained us knew any more about the subject than we did. Once we settled in Kabul, we learned that there was something called *"charss"* for sale in the bazaars, and we knew that there were often people in teahouses who seemed to be smoking *charss*. Some old men seemed to be addicted to it, or, at least, they spent most of their times in teahouses smoking it. But one did not see people smoking *charss* in the streets, and no one ever offered me any. It was all around us, actually, if we had wanted it, but it never occurred to us to even think about trying it.

Towards the end of my stay, I did get into a discussion with my students about *charss*, and they laughed and asked if I had ever tried it. It wasn't a big deal to them; they knew it made people feel and act a bit strange, but it was not forbidden, like alcohol. If they had tried alcohol, they would not have discussed that openly, just as young people in our culture don't discuss using pot, at least with adults. Cultural relativism, again.

I was interested enough in the subject so that some students eventually gave me a piece of *charss*. It was a stick, about three inches long, of a clay-like black substance. I went home, crumbled a little of it into my pipe tobacco (I was a pipe smoker from age eighteen until about fifty, when my kids convinced me to give it up), and smoked my pipe. As usual, I did not inhale, so I felt nothing. Yes, I was that stupid. I had no idea about inhaling, or I probably would have been more than stoned. The stick of *charss* was, I believe, pure hash, but unless you ingest or inhale hash, it's not going to do much for you. So I put it away and forgot about it, and a couple of years later I noticed it lying there with some other souvenirs I had brought home and realized that I had inadvertently smuggled in a good-sized chunk of contraband.

Since then the whole world has become aware of how terrible drugs are supposed to be, thanks to the wholly ineffective efforts of the United States DEA to eliminate drug usage. This is not the place to delve deeply into how and why our population has begun consuming drugs to a degree unknown when I was younger. It is worth a moment, however, to observe that our drug culture has international repercussions, some of which have changed Afghanistan.

If there were poppies cultivated in Afghanistan when I was there, I didn't know about it and, in any case, it must have been a small crop. Demand for opium-derived drugs was much less then, and the long-established fields of Turkey, Iran, and many other nations were sufficient to supply that demand. Transportation of anything into or out of Afghanistan was far more difficult than in those other poppy-raising countries, so it was not a likely exporter of drugs. Until there was a determined American effort to cut off drug supplies, thereby inflating the value of drugs, there was not much incentive for a crop of poppies larger than might be sufficient for the desires of the local population, like all other Afghan crops.

Four decades and untold millions of dollars later, a determination to designate some drugs as contraband has made the trade hugely profitable. It has also forced it to hide.

Nations like the U.S., with open societies and easy access to almost every patch of land, are not good places to raise secret crops requiring large fields. Marijuana can be, and therefore is, cultivated in small amounts, even indoors, or is brought in from countries to the south where it grows easily and oversight is difficult. Opium, however, must be grown where large fields can be hidden from authorities unless those authorities can be bribed efficiently. Consequently, South America has become prime source of opium derivatives. Our efforts to put down this drug traffic have had mixed results, depending often on how much money we are willing to extend governments to compensate for lost bribes, but one of those results has been the destabilization of the economies of several South American countries.

No surprise, then, that Afghanistan, where there is virtually no government control, has become a new focus of opportunity for opium farming. The very inadequacies of the transportation system become a plus; since bringing goods into or out of the country by truck, given the horrendous state of the roads, has long been almost impossible, smuggling of goods of all kinds has a long history there, and it is as easy to smuggle dope as anything else. Moreover, given the political realities of the country, control of most areas has always rested in the hands of tribal chiefs and warlords. With the breakdown of any national economy over the past decades, all that matters to most people is the local economy, the crops and products of small, immediate areas. Opium, if it can be smuggled out of the country, is not simply the most valuable crop one could produce, but probably the only exportable crop worth trying to export. All one needs is protection. That's what the local warlord can provide.

It is entirely possible that the only reason many Afghan families have survived during the recent years of civil war is that they could buy food with the proceeds of their drug crops. Our legislators may feel strongly about the evils of drug use, but for a farmer in a distant country whose family might starve without his crop, our feelings about the subject are of no importance. It is a matter of weighing the consequences for some people who choose a certain behavior against those who have no choice. Our moral stance, in that light, may seem like empty posturing.

It is almost inevitable that, unless the American people and government come to their senses one of these days and reconsider the effects of a long-failed drug war, we will be faced with a daunting decision sooner or later. With the Taliban no longer in control, some other government will need our assistance in putting Afghanistan back into a semblance of order. We will have to do that or face a continual future of one more Moslem nation with a poor, uneducated population, led by religious figures whose followers can find hope only in an afterlife because there is so little hope in this one. We have seen the results of having our own technology turned upon us by people who consider that technology oppressive, since it is not available to them in adequate amounts and with adequate infrastructure to improve their lives. After September 11, 2001, there cannot be many leaders in western nations who do not understand that their own freedom and security will depend on a rapid and massive change in the lives of millions of the world's poor.

Perhaps, someday, we will come to terms with our own desire for freedom, including the freedom to use drugs. We will find some way to reconcile our beliefs about ensuring the general good while preserving individual rights, even if those rights may be self-destructive. We will either create a general environment in which drugs are not desired, or we will learn to live with and control those desires to an adequate degree. Some would argue that we are already capable of doing the latter, were it not for beliefs which consider the use of some mind-altering substances immoral but characterize others, wine, for example, as sacred.

In the short run we will inevitably be faced with the fact that the drug trade in Afghanistan is there because of forces we set in motion. We have not diminished the use of drugs in our own nation, except for tobacco, a drug we continue to export to other countries. Interestingly, we do not seem to have that drug trade on our collective national conscience. We allow tobacco to be grown in our country because it supports some millionaires and a lot of ordinary people. Should we condemn to starvation whole villages of Afghans by trying to prevent them from cultivating a crop which, in the broad view, does less harm to fewer people in the world than our tobacco crops?

As I wrote at the beginning of this chapter, I was far more ignorant and innocent than I am today when I lived in Afghanistan. I hardly noticed that pot was sold openly and used in moderation, or that other drugs were available but not widely used. Neither I nor my fellow volunteers nor the government that employed us, nor the Afghan government, gave a lot of thought as to who used drugs, where, and why because it really didn't matter.

Forty years later, I think the whole world was wiser then to believe that and to act upon that belief by simply letting the drug trade alone, each country regulating its people to the degree they chose to be regulated. There were more drugs available in Afghanistan when I lived there than in the U.S., but they were no problem. They became a problem when our government began to perceive them as one. They now are a problem for the whole world. But it need not be that way.

We will need to help remake Afghanistan. One of the issues we must confront, in doing so, is the current dependence of many Afghan farmers on a crop our government wishes to destroy. Let us hope that this may spur our leaders to rethink how America has allowed itself to be caught up in an international war not on terrorism, which may be impossible to win, but on drugs, which we have already lost.

Whether our efforts to overcome terrorism by driving terrorists out of Afghanistan proves to be folly remains to be seen. We were attacked; our choices were limited; we cannot live safely or freely with the threat of terrorist attacks. On the other hand, our efforts to eliminate drug use have already proven futile. We could live safely and freely without waging war on drugs, as other societies and our own did for centuries. The war on drugs is an unjust and useless war. As our country faces an uncertain future of "war" against unseen enemies promising to terrorize us, it seems a good time to consider abandoning the absurdity of waging war on an international trade we cannot control and on a small segment of our own population with behaviors of which some disapprove.

Time

THE PEACE CORPS PROVIDED EACH HOUSEHOLD WITH a trunk full of books, including a complete set of the World Book Encyclopedia. I am not sure how the books were chosen; some were designed for adults and some for children, and it seemed as if they were not so much selected for any specific purpose as by whatever surplus books various publishers were willing to donate. But one book in the collection, The Silent Language by Edward T. Hall, was immediately relevant, entirely fascinating, and should be part of the education of anyone who wants to understand the differences between American culture and the many other cultures around the globe.

The silent language to which the book's title refers is the language of convention, assumptions about reality which are embedded in our upbringing and therefore seem "normal." They are actually entirely arbitrary. Take, for example, the distance which separates two people during conversation and the volume at which they converse. It is difficult to define these, but one certainly recognizes personal discomfort when speaking with someone who stands too close or who speaks too loudly. In Afghanistan, closer and louder is the standard, so that Americans speaking with Afghans could be observed engaged in an odd dance, the Afghan always stepping closer and the American retreating, each searching helplessly for a familiar comfort zone to share. Similar conventions exist about the distance one would stand, and the volume at which one would speak, when addressing a crowd. Speeches given by foreign leaders may often seem to us to be demagogic because they are so loud, but this is often simply a result of a different convention.

There are more complex conventions about the use of space, which one can best become aware of outside of the United States. In spite of, or because of, our tradition of "wide open spaces," Americans do not generally like crowds. We try not to touch strangers on a bus or in a subway. We try not to touch one other, even friends, when we are standing together. In many other countries where crowded conditions are unavoidable, standing in crowds does not cause discomfort. Whenever my fellow volunteers and I went to public events we felt stifled by the crowds around us. What was to us an established respect for distance between one's body and another person's body was, it seemed, a sign of unfriendliness, even hostility.

Spatial conventions aside, an even greater contrast existed with conventions regarding time. The way we perceive time is, after all, only partly dependent on observable events. A day is a day, certainly, since that period of time is fixed by the rotation of the earth, but an hour is an arbitrary division of that day, one which was impossible to even imagine until the creation of mechanical clocks and watches. Measuring a day by hours is a relatively recent event in human history; it seems obvious to us because we are so used to it, but it is only a convention. One could as easily divide a day into twenty periods, or ten, or any number at all, or simply into day and night, as most rural people have always done.

A month also has a certain validity as a measure of time, since it reflects the waxing and waning of the moon. Since the moon takes about 28 days in that cycle, a seven-day week is a logical division of that period; 28 is only divisible by 2, 4, 7, and 14, and of those numbers only 7 seems of the right size to form a useful sub-division within a month. Of course, that means that a year cannot be made up of an even number of weeks or moon-months, so we adjust the lengths of months and, every so often, the lengths of years. It comforts us to see these units as steady, repeating patterns, but they are not. A year, like a day, reflects a physical reality, one that has an effect on life, creating cyclical growth patterns for plants and migratory patterns for some animals. But there is no physical result from the passage of a week, or a month, and our feeling that something important has actually occurred because a week has elapsed is a social convention, not a reality.

The power of convention was illustrated vividly during the two years preceding and following the "millennium." That event was much discussed and celebrated; some ignorant religious types even expected earthshaking changes to occur. The millennium, though, is a simple convention of a particular calendar. That calendar has become commonly accepted by all nations, but the acceptance is a result of western commercial hegemony and nothing else. There was no millennium for Moslems, or for Orthodox Jews, or for Buddhists or Hindus, that is to say, for the majority of mankind. Nothing happened at all on January 1, 2001 (or January 1, 2000.) Nothing happened at midnight that day because there is no such thing as midnight except in a local sense. The middle of the night moves steadily across the globe, and it is only a generally accepted pretence (originally instituted by railroads in order to create schedules) that it occurs simultaneously throughout a particular time zone.

All this is obvious, yet we in western nations are still fixated on time conventions as if they were entirely real. We live our lives by clock and calendar, as our technology-driven culture requires. Exposure to a society which has only recently come in contact with a global view of reality forces us to understand that there are very different ways of dealing with time, ways that might be equally valid for people whose lives are not affected materially by the passage of an hour, a day, a week, a month, or even a year.

Our standard metaphorical view of time is that the future lies "ahead" of us. This seems so obvious that it comes as something of a shock to realize that the metaphor is constructed, not forced upon us. We are used to imagining time as something like an approaching freight train, full of empty boxcars which we look down upon from a bridge beneath which the train passes. We see the train coming from afar, but we don't know what those boxcars may contain until the train passes below us, in the present. If we can find out ahead of time about the contents of the cars, we can empty or fill them, use the contents or ignore them, and then, once they have passed us, they will recede behind us, no longer of much interest. Western culture, on the whole, tries to see into the future in order to control the present.

Now, change the way that metaphor is applied. Imagine that we are standing facing away from the same train as it approaches us from the rear. We cannot see what is in it, and so trying to plan how to use its contents is a pointless exercise. Only when it appears below us, in the present, do we know what that present contains, and as it recedes before us, into the past, we can make use of our knowledge of that past to better our lives in the present.

If the future is unknowable, then the past is what really matters and what one must study. We may see such a viewpoint as fatalistic, but each of us learns, as we grow older, that there is much wisdom in understanding and accepting what we cannot control and in taking a long, patient view of what it is we really can control. The events of September 11, 2001, were both terrifying and humbling; suddenly, we realized, that no matter how powerful a nation we were, we could not assume that we had any power to control our own future. Seemingly out of nowhere, a band of fanatics had upset many of our preconceptions and assumptions, and suddenly we would have to learn to live with a degree of doubt and uncertainty about what the future held beyond anything to which we had become accustomed.

One day in one of my classes in Kabul, I explained to my students that when I returned to America I would almost certainly have a pocket calendar to carry with me, each day of the month for the year to come printed out as a little box, and that I would schedule various events into those boxes. If a friend asked me if I had something to do, say, two weeks from then on a Thursday at four o'clock, I could probably tell him. This revelation produced the longest period of sustained laughter that I recall in my class. It was such a silly, frivolous idea, such a crazy and pointless assertion. It was impossible to understand except as some sort of weird joke.

For most Afghans, even those who went to work each day at an office and lived by some kind of schedule, time was not something which rules us. We do not use time. We float in it.

During my two years in Afghanistan, more often than not when I was asked to someone's house for dinner, the conversation went something like this:

"Please, I would like you to come to my house and have dinner with me."

"Thank you so much. When?"

"Now."

"But it is four o'clock. When do you want me to come for dinner?"

"It doesn't matter. Come with me now. We will have dinner later."

"But my servant is preparing dinner for me tonight already. Could I come tomorrow?"

"Please, come now. We would like you to come. We are expecting you."

"I am so sorry, but I planned to be at home tonight. My roommate and I are having dinner together."

"Don't you want to come? Please. It would be my pleasure."

Sometimes I went. Sometimes I did not. If I went, it did not turn out that anyone was expecting me, or that food had been purchased or plans made. It might be hours before dinner was served. Other people might come or might not, and dinner would be served whenever it seemed like a good idea. One does not plan to have dinner, or plan much of anything else, because planning implies that you can know what is going to happen in the future, or do something about it, and you can't really do either, as most Afghans see things.

Several years after I returned to the U.S., I received a telephone call from someone who had met me in Afghanistan and had since moved to a town about ten miles from my home. He wanted to invite me to dinner; he was thinking of starting an Afghan restaurant, he said, and wanted to try out his cooking. At this point in my life, I had put my Peace Corps experience behind me; I was married and starting a family, but I thought I should be polite and go, although my wife could not go with me. So I accepted, asking him what time I should arrive. "Seven o'clock," he said.

"I want to be sure I understand," I told him. "I know that Afghans often do not do things on a schedule, the way Americans do. You have been here for a while, so you know that when an American invites somebody for dinner at seven, he expects the guest to arrive around 7:15, and then they eat around 7:30 or maybe 8, if they have drinks first. So I would really like to know: do you really want me to come at 7, or 7:15, or much later? What time do you want to have dinner."

"I understand," he said. "I would like you to come at seven o'clock."

So, like an idiot, I showed up on his doorstep at 7 o'clock, to discover that he was not quite dressed, still shaving. I think we began dinner around 9.

We felt we should invite him to our house for dinner, so I warned my wife that he might well be very late. She is an excellent cook and wanted to serve a dinner that could not be slapped together at the last minute. I did explain to him exactly what time we planned to serve dinner and invited him to come a half-hour or so before that. Not only did he show up more than an hour later than the dinner time I had given him, but he brought his small child with him, which we had not planned for. We had a nice evening, but it ended much too late for either of us to feel clear-headed the next morning at work.

Picnics outside of Kabul were a favorite type of entertainment for Afghans, and our volunteers were regularly invited to many. They could begin as early as 7 a.m. Bob Pearson and I arrived at one around 10 a.m. Tea and cookies were served around 1 and the picnic lunch (an elaborate and excellent one, with various *pilaus*, breads, and fruits) served around 3. We left well before the "picnic" ended. We figured it would go on until it got dark. At one point, the Headmaster of my school decided that picnics for all the teachers would be a wonderful idea, promoting staff cohesion and appreciation. He thought twice a month would be about right. Since the work week lasted six days, Bob and I had a difficult time showing enthusiasm for giving up two of our four free days each month to sit and exchange small talk, very small talk, for ten or twelve hours, and fortunately the plan never came to fruition.

Our apartment was above a whole series of one-room, open front shops, most of which sold nearly identical goods. One shop in particular opened early ever day, about 6 a.m. We could tell it was open because the owner played his radio very loud, probably to share its programs with everyone else in the neighborhood. He closed up after dark, around 8. He had, it appeared, less than a dozen customers each day. Frank and I were struck by the amount of time this shopkeeper invested in doing so little. We figured he could have opened several hours later and closed several hours earlier and still easily served the small number of customers who came there regularly. He would have made no less money and spent far less time doing it.

My understanding of the Afghan view of time only came to maturity after a year or so. That was when Frank and I figured out why the shopkeeper spent so many hours doing so little. What else was there for him to do? If he had opened later or closed earlier, what could he have done with the time? He lived in the shop. His friends knew he was there. He could sit in front and listen to his radio, and see people walk by, and do a little business, and that was his life.

That was all his life had ever been and all it could ever be. He had a whole lifetime to do what he was doing, and so what time it was, or what day it was, or what year it was made no difference at all. It has made no difference at all to generations of other shopkeepers in that country and all over the world, for thousands of years. That's how most of the world is, even today. Whose view of time, all things considered, is the strange one?

We think that we can "spend" time. Most cultures realize that one can only experience it.

▼▼▼▼▼▼

Hats

▼▼▼▼▼▼▼

SOMETIMES TINY DETAILS CAN BE SUGGESTIVE. WATCHING videotapes of Afghanistan taken during the past two years and looking over my own collection of old slides and newspaper clippings eventually caused me to wonder about a very small detail and to draw some conclusions from it.

Where are all the *karakul* caps?

Karakul is the name given to the breed of sheep most common in Afghanistan. *Karakul* caps were the most common headgear in Kabul while I was there. They came in black, brown, gray, and golden tan, black being the most common and least expensive and gold being the rarest and most costly. Not only were certain colors more prized, but the tightness of the curl and the regularity of pattern of each fleece were also important matters of taste and sophistication. I daily wore a fairly common one I had purchased soon after arriving. Later, when I had agreed to tutor the daughter of an Afghan family (secretly, since they were in political disfavor at the time) to prepare her for college in America, she presented me with two beautiful *karakul* skins to have made into caps. I still own them.

The shape of a *karakul* cap is much like the type of cap Nehru wore, narrow, with a slight rise at the back. It did not come with ear flaps or extend far enough over the side of the head to afford any real protection during the winter cold. It was nowhere near as practical as a turban, which could be (and was) used to cover the face during a windstorm, to wipe the hands, and to provide warmth for the face and shoulders on cold days. *Karakul* caps were essentially ornamental signs of status, as hats have been in most civilizations. Our egalitarian culture has now given up hats almost entirely, but in my childhood all men wore hats, and there were distinct messages conveyed by them. Watch a movie filmed before World War II and notice how bowlers, Homburgs, straw boaters, derbies, military caps, and snap-brim jockey caps instantly suggest the age and status of the wearer. In Afghanistan, the *karakul* cap was an unacknowledged but clear status symbol. The only men who wore turbans were *mullahs* or old working men.

The children at my schools in Kabul often wore *karakul* caps, or sometimes cloth caps like those worn by golfers in the 1920s. They never wore turbans. They were children gaining an education, a sign of status in itself, so like educated men in the capital, they wore western clothes, mostly second hand ones from the bazaar. Second hand clothes from the west were cheaper than having traditional flowing garments made to order, so wearing them was not necessarily a sign of affluence or status. But the *karakul* cap, because it was a luxury, was. Even shopkeepers chose to wear them if they could afford to do so.

In the north, I found, the *karakul* cap was much less common, even though sheep raising was a major occupation there. The boys at my school in Mazar-i-Sharif wore a uniform with a military look to it, with a uniform cloth cap. I assumed that the school supplied these. Some of the teachers wore the *karakul* cap, but many of the teachers were *mullahs* who wore the turban. Shopkeepers often wore embroidered skullcaps, something one saw only occasionally in Kabul; these were more commonly worn by Tadjiks. There was also a flat rough brown cap which was worn all over Afghanistan. Known as the *"pakool,"* it seemed to be associated with Pushtun laborers or lower-class folk, but it now seems to be the favored headgear of most males, including even the Northern Alliance warriors, most of whom are not Pushtun. There is probably some sociological significance to this change, but all I know is that a change has taken place.

If this little essay on hats appears obsessive, it has a point. After the Taliban came to power, pictures from Afghanistan never showed anyone wearing a *karakul* cap. Western clothing had not disappeared entirely, but the *karakul* cap seemed to have vanished. It would be interesting to know exactly why this is the case.

One obvious explanation would be the Taliban's insistence on a return to life as it was when Islam was the predominant culture in much of the world. Afghan men were now required to wear their hair and beards long; shaving or cutting one's hair met with severe punishment. Perhaps there were also decrees about wearing only traditional clothing, including the turban. Just as requiring women to wear the *chadri* reduces them to a common appearance and robs them of individuality, so does requiring men to dress alike establish the kind of tyranny which typifies totalitarian states, religious or secular.

Absent a specific decree that outlawed the *karakul* cap, it might simply be the case that the entire class of people who used to wear them had either fled the country or wanted to remain out of sight. It was not my experience that wearers of the cap were necessarily the most educated or westernized, but Afghans who had familiarity with western attitudes and modes of thought were never seen wearing a turban. Many were people who had sought education abroad, returning to man government offices, technical jobs, transportation, industry, communications, finance, and all the infrastructure of a modern state. When the country was beset by civil war, many of them must have fled. As the country fell into the grip of a fanatic religious sect, more must have fled. There cannot be many men remaining in the country who would have worn the badge of the educated class in the past, and those who remain would not have reason to wear it.

It is a very small point, but it symbolizes one of the greatest barriers to Afghanistan's recovery from its current condition. There appears to be virtually no one left in the country with the training to do more than shoot an imitation Kalashnikov or a home-made Stinger missile. The armies of the Taliban were made up of ignorant, uneducated tribesman without any future in the modern world. No wonder they choose to live in the manner of Mongol invaders, a style of civilization which has long since been thrown into the dustbin of history. The armies opposing them were not as oppressive; even before the overthrow of the Taliban, girls could be educated, music could be played, and people could wear what they wished, living under the rule of the Northern Alliance. But the *pakool* seems to have replaced the *karakul* cap as an alternative to the turban. One suspects that soldiers of the Northern Alliance were not very different, in education and background, from Taliban soldiers, and thus not people who could afford to buy or would choose to wear *karakul*, even if it were available.

Afghanistan is Rome after Alaric, or Eastern Europe after Attila. Rome needed a millennium to recover (and its civilization was only preserved, incidentally, by Moslem scholars during the flourishing of their own civilization). It will take more than a decade or two before Afghanistan can climb back to a semblance of what it was only recently. But if it is to do so at all, it will require not only the help of other nations where civilization has been and is being preserved, including Moslem nations, and not only restoration of its infrastructure in the form of roads, canals, communications, schools, and light industry. It will take more than millions upon millions of dollars. It will take people, the return of the middle class to reclaim their country. It will require incentives for them to return and restore their lives and their lands. When we see people in Kabul wearing *karakul* caps again, we can begin to have some hope.

Shortly after the fall of Kandahar in December, 2001, Hamid Karzai was named acting head of the interim government agreed upon by the various representatives who had been meeting in Germany for several weeks to begin the process of putting the country back together again. Within a few days, his picture appeared in American papers. He was wearing a *karakul* cap. It was a good sign.

Standing in Line

S O MUCH THAT WE DO IS HABITUAL. LIVING IN A LAND with entirely different habits provides an education in cultural relativism which cannot be acquired in any other way. It also provides a perspective on some issues that our own nation has struggled with during the last few decades of the twentieth century.

We are a melting pot where not all elements have liquefied with ease. We are a nation of immigrants where some people whose ancestors arrived earlier remain more equal than others. We are a land of the free and home of the brave where the freedoms of some to dislike others often impinge on the freedom of all to feel safe and secure in maintaining their individual cultures.

We continue to engage in a national debate which pits political correctness against deeply held prejudices. We know we are supposed to allow others to do as they wish as long as their acts do not hurt others, but we still feel uneasy at some of those acts. In my city, San Francisco, Chinese Americans offering live animals for sale as food in the market place have been accused of cruelty. In feminist circles, the practice of female circumcision abroad (and possibly now in our own country) is anathema. In California, the use of Spanish as a second state language seems justified by the large population whose roots grew in Central and South America, yet many others feel threatened by the specter of bilingualism which has created tension elsewhere, as in Canada's French provinces. Some city governments in my state have tried to find ways to recruit workers who can speak the many languages of their citizens (Spanish, Chinese, Japanese, Lao, Vietnamese, Samoan, Filipino, to name only some) and faced objections from English-speaking job seekers who believe they have thus become the objects of discrimination.

The lessons one learns in a country like Afghanistan reveal how deep are the divisions between cultures, and how impossible it is to bridge those chasms without continued awareness of differences not easily perceived.

I take as a small example the Kabul Post Office. On my first visit there, I did what I would have done in any post office. I stood in line to buy stamps. I say I stood in line, but that is not exactly correct. There were no lines at the counters. There were groups of people, all pushing forward to try to get the clerk's attention. It was not a mob; people who arrived later than others did not try to shove others aside. Yet they did not stand in a line; they stood in a semi-circle, which I took to mean that there were, in effect, multiple lines which the clerk would attend to as best he could.

After a while, I did reach the counter when the person directly in front of me moved aside. It was someone next to me who was served first, but we had arrived at the counter at more or less the same time, and so I patiently waited. Then another person, further down the counter, was served, and although I wasn't sure he had really arrived at the counter before me, I still was on my best Peace Corps behavior and waited patiently.

Then someone reached over my head and dropped a letter on the counter in front of me, demanding service. And, just slightly, I lost it. There was no way that person could believe he was in front of me; it was, in my universe, simply a rude, thoughtless attempt to butt ahead, and I felt offended. It was obvious from the expressions on the clerk's face and on the face of the customer behind my shoulder that they hadn't the faintest notion what my problem was.

Later, when I became more experienced, I understood completely. At school, when I wanted to talk to the headmaster, it was very much the same situation. I would walk into his office to find him dealing with several people at the same time, all trying to get his attention, all thrusting at him whatever paper or letter they had, or trying to out-shout someone else for his attention. Nobody waited in a line outside his office. No one waited in a line inside, either. A line implies a "first-come, first-served," ethic. What I was observing was "the most important person is served first" ethic.

As an American with a college education, I was almost always acknowledged first at all my Afghan schools. The headmaster would defer to me, even if I stood back quietly and tried not to demand his attention. I was being granted status, whether or not I wanted it, and he was acquiring status by recognizing me.

Visitors to Great Britain have commented on the propensity there to form lines or "queues" for services. It has been said that if two Englishmen meet at a bus stop, the first thing they will do is to form a queue. There is probably an important lesson here: England has always been known as a society where social class is of great importance. For example, it was once essential to belong to the Church of England in order to have any real access to power. During the nineteenth century, as railroads brought the modern world to every part of the British Isles, as schools were created for the entire population, as growing literacy made possible newspapers and novels spreading new ideas to all classes, increasing equality of education necessitated opening advancement in politics to "dissenters," then to Catholics, then to Jews and freethinkers. The divisions between social classes became harder to discern. Everyone was now mixing in the city shops and in common transportation systems. Absent rigid customs requiring deference by some to others, forming lines to receive service is the only alternative to the kind of chaotic scrambling for attention which I observed in Kabul. In a society where other signs of status are ample, such as England's, it makes sense to find ways to grease the wheels of commerce. The absence of this behavior in Kabul, trivial though it may be, reveals a very different social history and social structure.

Another, more profound, behavior which characterizes Afghan society is the primacy of hospitality. A guest is shown every deference. Enter an Afghan home, and you will be invited to have tea or a meal and to stay as long as you wish. The younger men of the house may stand in your presence throughout your visit. Even shopkeepers will often invite you to have some tea, especially if you are going to be in the shop for a while to examine some of the goods. A foreigner invited to work in Afghanistan is a visitor and is therefore generally treated with similar deference all the time.

Jason Eliot reports a touching instance of this when he visited a jail near Herat where a prisoner had been held for years. The near-naked inmate's only possession was a small scrap of material on which he could sit to protect himself from the cold ground in his cell, so when Jason approached the cell, the man immediately arose and beckoned for him to take a seat on that one scrap. Visitors to Afghanistan even in recent times of famine and deprivation continue to remark upon being offered what little food a family may have whenever visiting an Afghan home.

The code of hospitality is enshrined in a specific tradition of the Pushtuns, known as the *pushtunwali*. Not exactly a code of law, but more than a simple tradition, the *pushtunwali* establishes a set of behaviors which preserve a semblance of civility for a set of tribes almost perpetually at war. The Pushtuns have a long history of inter-tribal struggle, as well as war with neighboring peoples who have sought control of the mountain passes between Central Asia and the Indian sub-continent. Western reporters have noted with surprise that the coalition of mujahedeen which ousted the Russians not only turned on one another after the Russians had left but have continued to break into antagonistic fighting units under warlords, changing sides for pay or for promises of mercy, ever since. In the city where I once spent months, Mazar-i-Sharif, it has been reliably reported that a Northern Alliance general switched sides and invited the Taliban in, then switched again and had them massacred, with the eventual result of a general massacre of the population when the Taliban returned. Such events perplex us; they seem to go against our understanding of any codes of honor. Yet these behaviors are not immoral when one understands the facts of life of a society in a state of constant internecine war. Changing sides to preserve one's forces and the lives of one's peoples makes more sense than fighting to the last man when all one is fighting for is a small piece of territory rather than a cause. Behavioral codes make sense when one understands the social realities that gave them birth.

I have emphasized the difficulties of travel in Afghanistan not simply to point out why military solutions to political problems are unlikely to succeed. When one has been a traveler in that barren and empty land, one understands why a cult of hospitality is a necessity.

Unless one feels some assurance of being welcomed and cared for when traveling, it would be unsafe to travel at all. Nobody would venture forth in a country where it is impossible to be assured of arriving at one's destination unless there was some feeling that other people will take care to assure protection for the helpless traveler. Again, I recommend Jason Eliot's book, an account of his wanderings, more often than not with little preparation or security, through war zones, along mined roads, across mountains, through gorges, always dependent on unanticipated means of transportation and lodging and, miraculously, always finding them. Most westerners would never dare travel in Afghanistan at all under the conditions Eliot faced. The lesson of his book is that Afghan traditions make such travel possible because, for centuries, conditions have been essentially the same as he encountered, and native traditions have evolved to overcome those conditions.

The presence of Osama Bin Laden in Afghanistan as a "guest" of the Taliban brought the issue of these traditions, and the code of *pushtunwali*, to international attention. Our government's demands that he be expelled from the country were seen as an unattainable request, violating the most sacred standards of protecting a guest.

Yet Osama was not quite a guest. He was invited into Afghanistan by foreign nations more than by the Afghan tribes. His money and the expertise of his followers were in demand in a time of war against the Russians. He was not invited for the purposes of waging war on Americans, Jews, and other Islamic regimes. He could claim to be a guest and certainly did so, and the Taliban, who were supported primarily by his financial resources, chose to deem him their guest. But other tribes, once the Taliban was overthrown, had no obligation towards him. The American policy of ousting the Taliban in order to cripple Bin Laden's organization (or possibly assassinate him) was certainly crafted with this in mind. Only when the Taliban could be rendered powerless would Bin Laden become an outsider rather than a guest and, as such, unable to claim sanctuary from his hosts. His former hosts would be dead, or powerless, or have changed sides to a different alliance.

A casual understanding of Afghan tradition might make Osama appear invulnerable, protected by the code of hospitality. A study of the many twists, turns, and betrayals of one tribe by another throughout Afghan history would suggest that codes of conduct are created not to deny reality but to allow civilizations to function. The Afghans have always found ways to survive, and when the key to survival becomes the replacing of one set of warlords with another, that is the path they must take. Bin Laden was essentially a foreign warlord; he is not Afghan, nor were most of his troops. His brand of Islam is not a common one. He was not owed any more protection than any other Moslem invader, of which there have been many.

After Bin Laden, or, rather after the Taliban, what can the role of United States be? That will depend largely on whether the advisers and volunteer workers we send there will be accepted as guests. It is crucial that we be invited by the Afghan government, and that the Afghan government is careful to invite only as many guests, and the right kinds of guests, as the country can tolerate. That was the situation when I served there; over a thousand Americans, as well as hundreds of Europeans, worked in Afghanistan to assist the government, and we were welcomed and treated well. It could become that way again. We must tread carefully and lightly in order to be invited as guests of Afghanistan, but if we can be welcomed, we will find that welcome, once again, warm, sincere, and whole-hearted.

▼▼▼▼▼▼

The Gods Must Be Crazy

▼▼▼▼▼▼

T HE INSANELY OPPRESSIVE BEHAVIOR OF THE TALIBAN
in the name of God need not be further
documented here. Religion has been a source of great
good and of stupefying evil throughout human history,
and current examples of men taking upon themselves the
authority of divine power in order to let loose their best
and worst impulses is not any different from the
massacres of Philistines by Hebrew tribesmen recorded
in the Old Testament, the periodic slaughter of Jews in
Europe in response to the Black Plague, the hundreds of
years of horrific warfare between Muslims and Christians
for control of worthless patches of "holy" land, or the
estimated deaths of one million innocent Hindus and
Muslims during the partition of India.

Yet in 1962, none of us who lived in Afghanistan would have
predicted the return to that country of the kind of primitive religious

fervor which, in a milder manifestation, had last dominated the land with the fall of King Amanullah in 1928. The triggering event which caused his expulsion and resulted in the nine-month reign of a bandit chief was said to have been the appearance of Amanullah's queen at a public gathering with her face unveiled, signaling a step into the modern world beyond what the common people would accept. But the common people have never been makers of Afghan history. What is more likely is that the revolt was a result of a series of missteps towards modernization by Amanullah and his advisors, his attempt to force a Loy Jirga to endorse his policies, an unpaid and undisciplined army ready to rebel, the arrest of highly respected mullah, and the underlying fact of Afghan politics: that no Afghan government has ever had much power outside of Kabul because of the realities of geography which fracture the land and prevent armies from controlling anything beyond the soil they actually occupy.

Outside of the cities, most of the population of Afghanistan has always been and is today without education or any information beyond what neighbors and friends supply. Radio (and television, before the Taliban forbade it) did bring a larger world into the countryside, but it is a mistake to assume that mere words out of the ether can change minds. They are more likely to be misunderstood or, more precisely, to be understood in a context we can hardly comprehend. If one has never known anything beyond a day's walk (in a land where a week's walk would not bring one to a different landscape), it is impossible to conceive of what is meant by a "country" or "nation" or "government" or "world."

This was best brought home to me by a discussion I had with a mullah at my school in Mazar-i-Sharif over lunch one day. He was a teacher there; I assume he had some education himself. "How did you get to Afghanistan?" he asked.

"I came on a plane," I answered.

He thought about this for a while. "Why didn't you take a bus?" he wanted to know.

I did not want to appear rude, so I explained as best I could. "The United States is very far away," I said. "And there is a big body of water, called an ocean (I had to use the English word, not knowing the Dari one) between our country and other countries."

"Certainly," he said. "I know this. But isn't there a bridge?"

When it came to bridges, incidentally, this mullah was not thinking of something like the Verrazano Narrows or the Golden Gate. I had been told that there was a bridge outside of Mazar, on the way to Maimana, which was very famous, and which I should see. I did see it, on an excursion to Balkh. We would call it a culvert.

In 1962, it was estimated that 90 to 95% of the population was illiterate. The first schools had been established by King Habibullah in 1903, and although slightly over one thousand schools were in operation by 1960, only about 10% of the students in rural primary schools got as far as fourth grade. Except for a tiny segment of the population, formal education did not exist at all outside the traditional teachings by mullahs in local mosques, those teachings confined to reciting the Holy Koran. Many of these teachers were themselves illiterate.

Thus, comparison of Afghanistan in 1962 to Medieval Europe is fitting, except that Europe had more large cities, more trade, better roads, and established systems of education. The mass of Europeans in the "dark ages" may have lived much the same lives as the mass of Afghans in the mid-twentieth century, their understanding of the universe a mixture of superstition, local tradition, and oral transmission of scriptures passed on by people who could not read the scriptures themselves. But in the lands which now comprise nations such as England, France, Germany, Italy, Spain, the Low Countries, and Scandinavia, the established religion was ruled from Rome through a hierarchical structure, no matter how imperfect it might be. Even the most ignorant village priest had a superior, somewhere, to whom he might turn for enlightenment. Islam is not a hierarchical religion. Lacking communication and transportation, rural mullahs have little more to rely on than what has been handed down to them from someone else.

The religious tyranny we see today is a product of such rural ignorance. There was no Taliban in 1962. It was a product of the recent creation of religious schools in Pakistan, from political and religious impulses having their origins in other countries. There was an entire population of young, ignorant men in the Afghan countryside who, having lived through years of civil war, had no livelihood and no future. The Taliban were created more by the grim circumstances of impoverishment and devastation than by any purely religious impulse. Like those Europeans who suffered through the Black Plague, famines, and the ravages of marauding armies and found scapegoats to kill, such as Jews and witches, the "fundamentalist" Moslems also seek scapegoats for the horrors they have suffered and find essentially the same ones: Jews and helpless women.

There was no question that Afghanistan was a Moslem country, and a very conservative one, when I lived there. There were no visible Hindu, Sikh, Buddhist, Christian, or Jewish communities. On the other hand, several such communities quietly and unobtrusively existed in the capital.

After the Taliban took over, they decreed that Hindus wear a distinguishing yellow ribbon, which indicates that there still were, and probably were when I was there, people who openly practiced Hinduism. Unlike the Pakistanis, the Afghans have no ongoing wars with Hindu neighbors, and thus no reason for antagonism; the Taliban may well have been influenced in this regard by Pakistani militants.

The Community Christian Church of Kabul was entirely a foreign establishment, patronized by expatriates of European nations working there, mostly Americans. The minister to this congregation was a gentlemanly and kind missionary type with the surprisingly apt name of J. Christy Wilson. He had worked in Kabul as a teacher at the American-run school, Habibiya, for about twelve years, and his Afghan students praised him for his kindness and skill. He displayed the best features of the devout missionary type, fully committed to his own brand of religion but selflessly serving others of different faiths. He was not universally liked by the foreign community because of his fundamentalism, but his detractors were mostly not Americans. I was surprised to discover so many Americans who were not simply practicing Christians but fundamentalists. Religious books and art were common in American homes. Some were not averse to commenting, privately, that the Afghan society was backward because of Islam, and that what was lacking was a spirit of brotherly love.

The government made no attempt to restrict these Christians' rights to hold services in the building which they had designated as their church. Small communities of Episcopalians, Catholics, and Mormons also held services. Any efforts at proselytizing the native population would have been extremely bad manners and possibly suppressed by the government, but, on the other hand, many upper class Afghans had lived abroad and were quite open-minded about spiritual matters and religious differences, so that there was no reason why private discussion of such matters could not take place, and it almost certainly did.

Personally, I never had students who showed interest in my religious beliefs, and I considered it prudent not to bring up the subject, especially because my own background is Jewish (although I have never practiced any religion or felt any desire to do so.) The only time I can remember anything resembling a discussion of religious practice coming up was when some students asked me how we buried our dead in my country. I wasn't quite sure what they meant; I had seen Afghan graveyards along the roadside, and I assumed that their practices were about the same as ours. I said we put the dead in the ground, usually in a box. I did not mention cremation, which I thought they might confuse with Hindu practices. But it turned out that what they really wanted to know was the position of the body when buried. They wondered if we buried people standing up. Apparently, some group does this, or they believed that some group does this, and they were relieved to hear that this was not something Americans considered.

I was very careful not to speak of Judaism at all, even though Afghanistan is far from Israel and was not then, as far as the government was concerned, strongly allied with the Arab nations demanding its destruction. But the existence of Israel, and the fact that its Moslem neighbors opposed that existence, had even then poisoned the atmosphere. On the only occasion I can recall the subject coming up (I do not recall why) I was speaking to someone in a shop who had said something about Jews. "What would you do if you met a Jew? " I asked him. "Kill him," was the response, but it seemed an instinctive one, not connected with any reality. As far as most Afghans knew, they never would meet a Jew.

Yet I did eventually learn that there was a small community of Jews in Kabul. One of the volunteers in our Afghan II group was a practicing Jew, not especially religious but still very conscious of being part of a people and a tradition. He set out to find if there was somewhere he could observe High Holy Days, and somehow he found that such a community existed in secret. Since he recognized that I was Jewish (in name, anyway) he invited me to join him. We made our way through some back alleys, as unobtrusively as possible, and found a house where, segregated into separate rooms, about fifty men and women were reciting and praying. My knowledge of Hebrew is non-existent, but my companion told me that their pronunciation had a distinctly Afghan accent. He also told me that this was a remnant of what was once a much larger community, descendants of immigrants from Russia or Persia in the previous century, and that most of the members were hoping to find some way to get to Israel eventually. Some of their Afghan friends must have known they were Jews, and they were not persecuted, but given the history of the last thirty years, I hope they all got out. (Acording to news reports, two Jews had somehow survived in Kabul to celebrate Hanukkah in 2001, but they were sworn enemies.)

My Peace Corps associate continued to keep in touch with his co-religionists, and on one occasion, about to leave for a vacation in Pakistan, he was asked to bring a can of coffee to some relatives there. It seemed an odd request, so although my friend agreed, he took the can home and opened it; it was not a sealed can, but simply a can filled with coffee, closed at one end with paper and tape. He carefully poured out the contents and found hidden there a small scrap of twisted paper with enigmatic writing on it. Were these directions to help move along a smuggling operation? Were they coded instructions from one spy to another? He couldn't tell, and my friend wasn't sure whether he should refuse to take the hidden message across the border (and thus admit to finding the message by violating a trust) or just make the delivery, risking getting caught as an accessory in some crime. Eventually, he pretended he didn't know anything about what was in the coffee and delivered it to the "cousins" in Pakistan, and received another package in return. Thus, whether or not that was his intention, he joined the "international Jewish conspiracy," a small but still living tradition of peoples isolated by unfriendly populations who remain in contact across borders in order to survive.

Everyone must know that Islam and Judaism are much closer in belief and practice than either of these religions is in relation to Christianity. The three arose from the same monotheistic impulses documented in the Old Testament, and in more ways than not, Mohammed's revelations were a reaction against the Christian version, which seemed to imply that God was tripartite, rather than a unity, and that God could have a mortal son. In Islam, as in Judaism, God is a unity beyond man's ability to comprehend. The five-times daily prayer of the devout Moslem begins with the affirmation that "there is no God but God," not remarkably different from the Jewish statement of faith, "Hear, oh Israel, the Lord our God, the Lord is one." Like Jews, Moslems circumcise their boys (although at adolescence, not a week after birth). Like Orthodox Jews, they abhor pork. They sometimes name their children from Old Testament sources: Daud (David), Isaq (Isaac), Ibrahim (Abraham), Yaqub (Jacob), and other common Afghan names are Hebrew in origin, although Mohammed, Achmad, Ali, Hussain, and other names from Islamic history are more common. Abraham is considered an ancestor of Moslems, and the place of his near-sacrifice of Isaac is identified as the same rock, enshrined as Jerusalem's Dome of the Rock, from which Mohammed ascended into heaven on his mystical night flight. Jesus is viewed as an important Jewish prophet. Mary is a familiar and comforting figure; girls are often named for her (Miriam.)

How can it be, therefore, that Jews and Moslems perceive one another as implacable enemies, while Christians (and Buddhists, Hindus, Parsis, atheists and agnostics) are left on the sidelines to deplore our modern religious warfare?

Afghanistan's recent history helps us see how the underlying causes of religious hatred have nothing to do with worship of God and everything to do with competition for space, food, clothing, and freedom of movement. Religion is the excuse for some individuals to do what they wanted to do in the first place. It was the excuse for the first Moslems to conquer most of Asia and much of Europe; it was the excuse for Christian Crusaders to try to recapture the Middle East and its rich trade routes. It has always been an excuse to appropriate the wealth of successful minorities. It has been the excuse, since the days of the Old Testament, for one people or another to insist on occupying the lands known as Judaea, Palestine, and Israel.

Afghanistan has been a crossroads. Most religions have been practiced there. There is even one small corner of the country, now called Nuristan (land of the new) that was previously called Kafiristan (land of the unbelievers) until it was subdued a century ago and its unique religious practices, probably a form of animism, terminated. Kabul was also the birthplace of Babur, founder of the Mogul Empire, where complete religious tolerance was practiced under one of its greatest rulers, Akbar. In times of stability and peace, Afghanistan has allowed people to do as they desired. In times of war, intolerance has promoted mass killings and cruelty. Here, as in other lands, one must recognize that the religion practiced under the Taliban was fanaticism, not "fundamentalism." Fundamental Islam requires prayer, fasting, helping the others, and pilgrimage, not slaughter and oppression.

Fanaticism is the child of sustained desperation. The only cure for desperation is to eliminate its causes: poverty, disease, ignorance, and hopelessness. Islamic fanatics oppose the modern world and all it stands for because they see it as a competitive religion of consumer-driven greed and materialism. In a sense, they are right, for material comfort is the one thing which can destroy fanatic, desperate men who assert spiritual authority when others have nothing else to turn to.

Our country has the means to slowly build a world where all people can live in comfort. Whether or not doing so is a religious mission, it is the only sure guarantee of our own religious freedom. Establishing freedom from want everywhere, even if it is not a religious obligation, is a practical and necessary antidote to the religion of hate which confronts us and the only way we can guarantee for ourselves the other freedoms we cherish.

Terrorism Began With Statues

I REMEMBER MY STUNNED REACTION WHEN I LEARNED that the Taliban had destroyed the statues of Buddha in the Bamiyan Valley. I should have been more than stunned; I should have understood, as I now do, what that foretold.

Bamiyan was one of the places to which Afghans proudly brought visitors. The ancient colossi towering over the valley were wonders of the world, though unfamiliar to most travelers. The Afghan people and its government, like any civilized people, preserved them as best they could, although they represented a religious tradition which had disappeared from their land over a thousand years before. Islamic leaders never would have thought of destroying them any more than they would have destroyed the objects in the Kabul Museum which documented Afghanistan's long history of visitation by multitudes of cultures and faiths.

It was not an easy trip to Bamiyan. It required a commitment of a couple of days, since the Bamiyan Valley is deep in the mountains at the center of the country. The trip had several sites worth seeing, however. In addition to the typical rocky, narrow gorges, there were two sets of ruins of unusual interest. They needed to be pointed out; a casual traveler might not notice that there was more to see than another pile of rocks. One pile, known as the Red City, was the ruin of a once-impressive city on a hilltop, where guard towers and walls were still discernible. The Red City had been attacked and captured by Ghengis Khan. Nearby was another ruin, this one showing no walls, no guard towers, no hint that people had lived there. It was known as the "Silent City," and the story told was that Ghengis Khan's son had been killed during the assault on the Red City. In retaliation, the Silent City had been reduced to rubble, its inhabitants all killed, its civilization entirely destroyed. That was centuries ago. It might be just a story. But that's certainly the way it looked. Even the Taliban were not as ruthless as Ghengis Khan is reliably reported to have been.

The hotel in Bamiyan was primitive, but relatively clean and comfortable by standards of the time and the country. The valley at its doorstep, on the day I visited, was green from the spring rains, edged with tall, slender trees whose leaves were just emerging.

The valley has tall cliffs along one side, and in the cliffs are the remains of what was once one of the most important centers of Buddhism. Caves riddle those cliffs, caves where monks once lived and pilgrims once visited. Paintings in the caves have been badly damaged through neglect in the centuries since Islamic invaders drove the Buddhists further east. But it is clear that this was a thriving, large community, where a religion born in India, far to the southeast, migrated, fermented, and spread to other regions along the Silk Road.

The truly impressive remnants of that civilization were the two giant Buddhas carved into the cliffs. Each had been created by cutting a huge niche, leaving a sculpture as a sort of giant bas-relief within that niche. Plasterwork had been added on for decoration, to simulate some of the draperies and hair. Paintings on plaster remained, in fragmentary form, in the arches above the heads. The smaller Buddha was slightly better preserved, but both were impressive. The large one was supposed to be the largest sculpture in the world, and although it was not freestanding, it was still hugely impressive. The Colossus of Rhodes is sometimes claimed to have been large enough so that ships could sail between its legs, and while these statues did not have separated legs, they were far taller than a modern cruise ship. One hundred seventy-five feet was the height claimed, about the height of a twenty-story building in a country which even today has no buildings near that height.

Islamic repulsion with idols had already taken its toll, centuries earlier. The faces of the Buddhas had been cut off; one could still see ears and hair, and the shape of the heads, but where human features once existed there was only a blank, vertical cut. But either because destruction of the Buddhas was too difficult or, more likely, because destruction of such amazing reminders of human achievement would be unconscionable, the statues had otherwise been left intact, ravaged only by time.

Islam has its roots in Judaism and Christianity, of course, and like some sects within those faiths it rejects worship of images. But just as those related faiths respect the practices of others, so does Islam.

The smashing of what are viewed as idols has always been the act of extremists, whether we are thinking of the ancient Hebrews in Canaan or Protestant iconoclasts. Just as the worshipers of the idols of Baal were, according to scripture, put to death by those who hated those idols, just as Protestants and Catholics who were willing to destroy each other's churches and were soon to try to destroy one another, just as Hitler first destroyed synagogues and later destroyed those who had worshipped there, it can come as no surprise that those who would destroy symbols of a different human faith would soon wish to destroy other humans.

When it was announced that the Taliban was determined to destroy the Buddhas with rockets and shells, the whole world protested. Other Islamic nations decried such pointless desecration of an antique treasure. It was as if Christians decided to smash the Venus de Milo because it represented a pagan goddess, or as if Michelangelo's David were to be destroyed by a sect disgusted by male nudity. It was an act of pure malice against alien thought and art, an assertion of the ability of vandals to destroy whatever they decided to hate, no matter what the opinion of the rest of mankind might be. It was simple barbarism. And months later, the much greater barbarism of destroying the World Trade Center and its occupants followed, derived from the same impulse of hatred.

It is less well known that the Taliban did not only destroy the great Buddhas of Bamiyan; they also visited the Kabul Museum and smashed every object of ancient art they could find. Curators wept as small, brittle pieces which had been carefully preserved for centuries were turned to powder by rifle butts. The Kabul Museum was small; there was little money available to preserve its holdings, and much had already been looted during the years of civil war. Nevertheless, it did hold a few priceless treasures, but because these were depictions of the human form, they were deemed to be a sacrilege in a pure Islamic nation, even though a thousand years of Islamic rule had not so deemed these treasures.

I do not mean to minimize the difference between what the Taliban did in Afghanistan and what was done in New York. One was an atrocity against history; the other was an atrocity against mankind. But the impulses for both are the same. If any person, or any sect, can come to the conclusion that an ancient piece of art is so offensive that it must be destroyed, it is actually but a small step to decide that people who practice and believe differently must, ultimately, be destroyed. .

After all, art is passive. It is no threat to anyone. One does not have to view it. One does not have to deal with it at all. It takes a deranged attitude to attack a piece of art, and in our lifetimes, only madmen have done so. When the Taliban decided to blow up part of the history of their own country, something which Afghans, a tolerant and hospitable people, have cared for over centuries, they declared themselves madmen.

The madmen's friends and associates took the next step in New York and Washington, and plan to continue. They have destroyed symbols of a culture they hate, along with thousands of people who happened to be in the way of that destruction.

As our nation still tries to make sense out of the horrors that occurred on September 11, we would do well to understand the nature of what we must confront. We are confronting the same kinds of murderous impulses which descended on and eventually brought down the Roman Empire, an empire which, like our own, was guilty of excesses but whose destruction left behind a period of darkness spreading over civilization for centuries.

This is not to say that those who attacked the World Trade Center did not feel they had honest grievances with the United States. It is not to argue that some of their grievances may even have been well founded. It is certainly not to label Moslems, or developing countries, or the dispossessed of any nation as supporting terrorism. Our country has had to look within as well as without to better understand how our foreign policies, and how religious zeal, and how cultural differences could have brought the world to confront terror as a political act. Politics does, on occasion, lead to war, and terrorism as a form of war is not something new. But what is new to us is the assertion of righteousness on the part of the terrorists, the assertion that because of the wrongs they feel they have suffered, God blesses their actions.

There is no point in arguing politics, or justification, or right and wrong with barbarians. Whatever their agenda, the destruction of the

Buddhas, like the destruction of the World Trade Center, went beyond any possible moral justification.

The new barbarians do not care about our culture, or our beliefs, or our opinions. Sadly, there is really no point in trying to find ways to accommodate them. We can be more accommodating as a nation, certainly, to the needs of other nations; in fact, we must do that. We have for too long turned our backs on other civilizations in too many ways. But the line which we must now draw is between civilization and barbarism. Barbarism is our enemy. Only barbarians blow up humanity's artistic treasures, and only barbarians destroy, with no guilt, people holding views they characterize as opposed to God.

It started with an attack on statues. Now it is an attack on civilization and those who create it. The statues in Bamiyan stood for over a thousand years and were wiped out in a few moments. The World Trade Center stood for only a few decades, but it was wiped out even more completely than the statues. We are confronting raw, mindless destruction, nothing less, and there can be no compromise with such impulses. Our response goes to the heart of what civilization is and what freedom must always be but, sadly, it is a response which seems to have no conclusion. There is no end to the worst impulses of mankind. There can be no end to the struggle against them

Lessons

I BEGAN THIS BOOK WITH THE INTENTION OF WRITING something to entertain while shedding light on a part of the world and on patterns of culture which few Americans have experienced. I was not certain that my experiences so long ago would speak clearly to today's issues, but as I continued writing, looking at my old journals and letters, I found that my own perceptions were being changed. Certain patterns emerged, current events stirred echoes of past events, and experiences which I had essentially forgotten suddenly presented themselves in a new and revealing light.

I began this book not as an expert, but as someone with strong memories long placed on the shelf while my life went on. The process of writing about these memories forced me to reexamine them and find new insights which I did not fully understand back when those events were only episodic occurrences, little more than part of an adventure.

I also began writing this book without a definite plan, without even a simple narrative thread. Instead, I typed out descriptions of trips, or tasks, or places, or perceptions in no particular order, as they came to mind. Later, having to give coherence to the material, I had to decide what might constitute chapters and in what order they would occur. It was the necessity of giving order to the material that forced me to notice how certain issues and themes emerged, themes which not only help to understand Afghanistan but to understand ourselves.

One obvious theme was how geography determines history, not an original observation. In the case of Afghanistan, the knot of mountains at the country's center, surrounded mostly by high desert or marginal grazing land, has dictated that Afghanistan will always be a nation in name only. For thousands of years, it has been a zone where cultures from the Indian sub-continent, from the Persian deserts, and from the great plains of central Asia have clashed. Conquerors have crossed the mountains and exercised control of territories surrounding the Hindu Kush, but this control has never knit the peoples of those lands together for long. It is a myth that Afghanistan has never been conquered; on the contrary, it has been conquered by every famous war machine marching across Asia. But the conquerors never stayed for long. There was no reason to stay. The land does not hold any treasure. It occupies mountains that separate civilizations, but the passes through them can only be held by the people who live there. There is nothing to entice peoples from other lands to settle permanently and hold the land.

Afghanistan has on rare occasion been compared to Switzerland. The comparison is of interest, as is the contrast. Like Afghanistan, Switzerland is multi-lingual. It is mountainous. It has been a crossroads for invading armies. But here the contrast becomes clear. Although multilingual, Switzerland ceased being tribal centuries ago. Although mountainous, travel and trade long ago became common with advances in technology. And most armies determined to go around Switzerland, not through it; it became obvious to powers governing Switzerland's neighbors that the price in blood and riches of holding the country would be too high to pay.

It is likely that Afghanistan was once as fertile as Switzerland today. Switzerland has one of the highest standards of living in Europe but has been spared the ravages of invasion. Whether because of climatic change, or because of deforestation centuries ago, or both, the standard of living in Afghanistan has been so low for so long that one must wonder why anyone would choose to invade it. Yet many nations have done so. What were their reasons, and what might be our own?

Not being an historian or an expert in geopolitics, I cannot pretend competence to evaluate our nation's foreign policy for the present or future. That is not my intent. Instead, I ask the reader to notice how easily we assume that, with enough effort, we can create a rational policy that will assure the future we desire. Such an attempt is a typically American, or Western, way of viewing the world.

We see history as a long story, with early causes bringing on later effects. In the history texts we prepare for our children, we write that story as if it was a coherent one, an uplifting account of events leading to better and better conditions, culminating in the wealth and comfort of our own country. But, of course, history does not have a plot. Men make history, and men try to strive for a world of greater comfort for themselves and their children, but as often as not, events take unexpected turns, wars and natural disasters intervene, civilizations arise and fall, and it is only our brief and blinkered viewpoint which creates the illusion of progress. For cultures much older than ours, it is all dependent on God's will, an unknowable mass of events whose pattern no human can perceive.

For two years I confronted the differences between American and Afghan perceptions of and uses of time, from the trivial differences of social conventions to the endless frustrations of attempting to travel anywhere according to a schedule. We view time as a current. Afghans view time more as a lake. Americans "go with the flow", trying to direct that flow into productive channels. But if there is no flow, if time is only the medium in which we exist, then wisdom and tranquility are to be found in acceptance of how things are and contentment with how things will always be.

Further, if time does not flow, but simply exists, then history is not a sequence of meaningful events, and the future can neither be predicted nor planned. History is only a recording of happenings, some of which have unique significance. In the view of many Islamic scholars, God spoke to Mohammed once. That was a unique event. Nothing that has occurred since or will occur in the future has more meaning that what happened then, so wisdom lies only in knowing as much as possible about what happened then, and why. From this perspective, to try to control the future is to assume the role of God, an obvious folly.

The Afghan culture understands, often with greater wisdom than our own, that control of our fate is limited. September 11, 2001, may someday be viewed as the day when Western civilization was forced to

accept that there is no such thing as absolute safety or absolute security or absolute control of our destinies. Technology, free trade, capitalism, and freedom of the human spirit from ancient tyrannies of class and religion have remade the world, yet primitive ignorance and brutality, armed with modern weaponry, can still bring civilization to a halt. Suddenly, we experienced the kind of shock that was felt by the Egyptians when the Hyksos overran their kingdom, or the Chinese Empire when the Mongols descended upon them. It is only because we are such a young nation that the sudden confrontation of a mighty civilization by ignorant hordes appears to be a novel event. Too often in the past, the ignorant hordes have eventually won, and if we hope to avoid those consequences, we might do well to become more familiar with the past and less fixated on the future.

It would be an absurd oversimplification to suggest that all Afghans view the world as unpredictable or that all Americans view the future as their plaything to shape to their wills. Within both cultures there are deep divisions of belief, ultimately based on religious precepts about God and the meaning of life. Every country has both religious fundamentalists and libertarian freethinkers. Religious doctrine can encompass doubt and free exploration, and atheism can harbor unyielding dogmatism. Still, the essential contrast of world-views is an enlightening one. The Afghanistan I knew was searching for ways to accommodate the world of technology, international communication and understanding, tolerance, and change. The Afghanistan of the Taliban rejected all of these, as do groups within our own nation who, certain of the absolute truths of ancient scriptures, can only see, as Afghan women were forced to see until recently, through a mesh which screens out most of the world about them.

I conclude by extending that metaphor. A person, even an entire nation, may don the *chadri*, a garment intended to protect its wearer by limiting that wearer's exposure to the realities of life. Or it may refuse to allow the *chadri* to be enforced on unwilling wearers and encourage all people to assert their rights to see whatever they wish (and be seen, openly, by others). One must note that the *chadri's* "protection" is enforced only on females, the half of humanity perceived to be weaker and in greater need of such protection. Protecting the weak is a virtue, but that is not the same as protecting them in order to maintain their inferiority, and that inferiority is not only the result but often the intention of such protection.